PERSONAL RECOLLECTIONS OF
JOAN OF ARC

PERSONAL RECOLLECTIONS OF
JOAN OF ARC

BY

THE SIEUR LOUIS DE CONTE

TRANSLATED BY

JEAN F RANCOIS ALDEN

EDITED BY

MARK TWAIN

(SAMUEL LANGHORNE CLEMENS)

IN TWO VOLUMES

VOL. II

GYAN

Published by

Gyan Publishing House
5, Ansari Road
Daryaganj, New Delhi-110002
Phone: 011-47034999, 9811692060
E-mail: books@gyanbooks.com

Distribution Network
gyanbooks.com
India, USA, Canada, UK, Australia

ISBN: 978-81-212-5510-3 (Set)
978-81-212-5512-7 (HB)
First Published, 1896

2nd Impression 2024

Printed at: Gyan Press, Delhi.

PERSONAL RECOLLECTIONS OF JOAN OF ARC (VOL. II)
Editor: MARK TWAIN, Translator: JEAN FRANCOIS ALDEN

PERSONAL RECOLLECTIONS OF JOAN OF ARC

Joan signs the list of accusations

PERSONAL RECOLLECTIONS

OF

JOAN OF ARC

BY

THE SIEUR LOUIS DE CONTE
(Her Page and Secretary)

FREELY TRANSLATED OUT OF THE ANCIENT FRENCH INTO MODERN ENGLISH
FROM THE ORIGINAL UNPUBLISHED MANUSCRIPT IN THE
NATIONAL ARCHIVES OF FRANCE

BY

JEAN FRANCOIS ALDEN

IN TWO VOLUMES

VOL. II

NEW YORK AND LONDON
HARPER & BROTHERS PUBLISHERS
1904

ILLUSTRATIONS

PHOTOGRAVURE

CONTENTS

CHAPTER XXVIII.

THE troops must have a rest. Two days would be allowed for this.

The morning of the 14th I was writing from Joan's dictation in a small room which she sometimes used as a private office when she wanted to get away from officials and their interruptions. Catherine Boucher came in and sat down and said:

"Joan, dear, I want you to talk to me."

"Indeed, I am not sorry for that, but glad. What is in your mind?"

"This. I scarcely slept last night, for thinking of the dangers you are running. The Paladin told me how you made the duke stand out of the way when the cannon-balls were flying all about, and so saved his life."

"Well, that was right, wasn't it?"

"Right? Yes; but you stayed there yourself. Why will you do like that? It seems such a wanton risk."

"Oh, no, it was not so. I was not in any danger."

"How can you say that, Joan, with those deadly things flying all about you?"

Joan laughed, and tried to turn the subject, but Catherine persisted. She said:

"It was horribly dangerous, and it could not be necessary to stay in such a place. And you led an assault again. Joan, it is tempting Providence. I want you to make me a promise. I want you to promise me that you will let others lead the assaults, if there *must* be assaults, and that you will take better care of yourself in those dreadful battles. Will you?"

But Joan fought away from the promise and did not give it. Catherine sat troubled and discontented awhile, then she said:

"Joan, are you going to be a soldier always? These wars are so long—so long. They last forever and ever and ever."

There was a glad flash in Joan's eye as she cried:

"This campaign will do all the really hard work that is in front of it in the next four days. The rest of it will be gentler—oh, far less bloody. Yes, in four days France will gather another trophy like the redemption of Orleans and make her second long step toward freedom!"

Catherine started (and so did I); then she gazed long at Joan like one in a trance, murmuring "four days—-four days," as if to herself and unconsciously. Finally she asked, in a low voice that had something of awe in it:

"Joan, tell me—how is it that you know that? For you do know it, I think."

"Yes," said Joan, dreamily, "I know — I know. I shall strike — and strike again. And before the fourth day is finished I shall strike yet again." She became silent. We sat wondering and still. This was for a whole minute, she looking at the floor and her lips moving but uttering nothing. Then came these words, but hardly audible: "And in a thousand years the English power in France will not rise up from that blow."

It made my flesh creep. It was uncanny. She was in a trance again — I could see it — just as she was that day in the pastures of Domremy when she prophesied about us boys in the war and afterward did not know that she had done it. She was not conscious now; but Catherine did not know that, and so she said, in a happy voice:

"Oh, I believe it, I believe it, and I am so glad! Then you will come back and bide with us all your life long, and we will love you so, and so honor you!"

A scarcely perceptible spasm flitted across Joan's face, and the dreamy voice muttered:

"Before two years are sped I shall die a cruel death!"

I sprang forward with a warning hand up. That is why Catherine did not scream. She was going to do that — I saw it plainly. Then I whispered her to slip out of the place, and say nothing of what had happened. I said Joan was asleep — asleep and dreaming. Catherine whispered back, and said:

"Oh, I am so grateful that it is only a dream! It sounded like prophecy." And she was gone.

Like prophecy! I knew it *was* prophecy; and I sat down crying, as knowing we should lose her. Soon she started, shivering slightly, and came to herself, and looked around and saw me crying there, and jumped out of her chair and ran to me all in a whirl of sympathy and compassion, and put her hand on my head, and said:

"My poor boy! What is it? Look up and tell me."

I had to tell her a lie; I grieved to do it, but there was no other way. I picked up an old letter from my table, written by Heaven knows who, about some matter Heaven knows what, and told her I had just gotten it from Père Fronte, and that in it it said the children's Fairy Tree had been chopped down by some miscreant or other, and —

I got no further. She snatched the letter from my hand and searched it up and down and all over, turning it this way and that, and sobbing great sobs, and the tears flowing down her cheeks, and ejaculating all the time, "Oh, cruel, cruel! how could any be so heartless? Ah, poor Arbre Fée de Bourlemont gone — and we children loved it so! Show me the place where it says it!"

And I, still lying, showed her the pretended fatal words on the pretended fatal page, and she gazed at them through her tears, and said she could see herself that they were hateful, ugly words — they " had the very look of it."

Then we heard a strong voice down the corridor announcing:

" His Majesty's messenger — with dispatches for her Excellency the Commander-in-Chief of the armies of France!"

CHAPTER XXIX.

I *KNEW she had seen the vision of the Tree.* But when? I could not know. Doubtless before she had lately told the King to use her, for that she had but one year left to work in. It had not occurred to me at the time, but the conviction came upon me now that at that time she had already seen the Tree. It had brought her a welcome message; that was plain, otherwise she could not have been so joyous and light-hearted as she had been these latter days. The death-warning had nothing dismal about it for her; no, it was remission of exile, it was leave to come home.

Yes, she had seen the Tree. No one had taken the prophecy to heart which she made to the King; and for a good reason, no doubt; no one *wanted* to take it to heart; all wanted to banish it away and forget it. And all had succeeded, and would go on to the end placid and comfortable. All but me alone. I must carry my awful secret without any to help me. A heavy load, a bitter burden; and would cost me a daily heart-break. She was to die; and so soon. I had never dreamed of that. How could I, and she so strong and fresh and young, and every day earning a new right to a peaceful and honored old age? For at that time I thought old age valuable. I do not know why, but I thought so. All young people think it, I believe, they being ignorant and full of superstitions. She had seen the Tree. All that miserable night those ancient verses went floating back and forth through my brain:

"And when in exile wand'ring, we
Shall fainting yearn for glimpse of thee,
Oh, rise upon our sight!"

But at dawn the bugles and the drums burst through the dreamy hush of the morning, and it was turn out all! mount and ride. For there was red work to be done.

We marched to Meung without halting. There we carried the bridge by assault, and left a force to hold it, the rest of the army marching away next morning toward Beaugency, where the lion Talbot, the terror of the French, was in command. When we arrived at that place, the English retired into the castle and we sat down in the abandoned town.

Talbot was not at the moment present in person, for he had gone away to watch for and welcome Fastolfe and his re-enforcement of five thousand men.

Joan placed her batteries and bombarded the castle till night. Then some news came: Richemont, Constable of France, this long time in disgrace with the King, largely because of the evil machinations of La Tremouille and his party, was approaching with a large body of men to offer his services to Joan — and very much she needed them, now that Fastolfe was so close by. Richemont had wanted to join us before, when we first marched on Orleans; but the foolish King, slave of those paltry advisers of his, warned him to keep his distance and refused all reconciliation with him.

I go into these details because they are important. Important because they lead up to the exhibition of a new gift in Joan's extraordinary mental make-up — statesmanship. It is a sufficiently strange thing to find that great quality in an ignorant country girl of seventeen and a half, but she had it.

Joan was for receiving Richemont cordially, and so was La Hire and the two young Lavals and other chiefs, but the Lieutenant-General, D'Alençon, strenuously and stubbornly opposed it. He said he had absolute orders from the King to deny and defy Richemont, and that if they were overridden he would leave the army. This would have been a heavy disaster, indeed. But Joan set herself the task of persuading him that the salvation of France took precedence of all minor things — even the commands of a sceptred ass; and she accomplished it. She persuaded him to disobey the King in the interest of the nation, and to be reconciled to Count Richemont and welcome him. That was statesmanship; and of the highest and soundest sort. Whatever thing men call great, look for it in Joan of Arc, and there you will find it.

In the early morning, June 17th, the scouts reported the approach of Talbot and Fastolfe with Fastolfe's succoring force. Then the drums beat to arms; and we set forth to meet the English, leaving Richemont and his troops behind to watch the castle of Beaugency and keep its garrison at home. By and by we came in sight of the enemy. Fastolfe had tried to convince Talbot that it would be wisest to retreat and not risk a battle with Joan at this time, but distribute the new levies among the English strongholds of the Loire, thus securing them against capture; then be patient and wait — wait for more levies from Paris; let Joan exhaust her army with fruitless daily skirmishing; then at the right time fall upon her in resistless mass and annihilate her. He was a wise old experienced general, was Fastolfe. But that fierce Talbot would hear of no delay. He was in a rage over the punishment which the Maid had inflicted upon him at Orleans and since, and he swore by God and Saint George that he would have it out with her if he had to fight her all alone. So Fastolfe yielded, though he said they were now risking the loss of everything which the English had gained by so many years' work and so many hard knocks.

The enemy had taken up a strong position, and were waiting, in order of battle, with their archers to the front and a stockade before them.

Night was coming on. A messenger came from the English with a rude defiance and an offer of battle. But Joan's dignity was not ruffled, her bearing was not discomposed. She said to the herald:

"Go back and say it is too late to meet to-night; but to-morrow, please God and our Lady, we will come to close quarters."

The night fell dark and rainy. It was that sort of light steady rain which falls so softly and brings to one's spirit such serenity and peace. About ten o'clock D'Alençon, the Bastard of Orleans, La Hire, Pothon of Saintrailles, and two or three other generals came to our headquarters tent, and sat down to discuss matters with Joan. Some thought it was a pity that Joan had declined battle, some thought not. Then Pothon asked her why she had declined it. She said:

"There was more than one reason. These English are ours — they cannot get away from us. Wherefore there is no need to take risks, as at other times. The day was far spent. It is good to have much time and the fair light of day when one's force is in a weakened state — nine hundred of us yonder keeping the bridge of Meung under the Marshal de Rais, fifteen hundred with the Constable of France keeping the bridge and watching the castle of Beaugency."

Dunois said:

"I grieve for this depletion, Excellency, but it cannot be helped. And the case will be the same the morrow, as to that."

Joan was walking up and down just then. She

laughed her affectionate, comrady laugh, and stopping before that old war-tiger she put her small hand above his head and touched one of his plumes, saying:

"Now tell me, wise man, which feather is it that I touch?"

"In sooth, Excellency, that I cannot."

"Name of God, Bastard, Bastard! you cannot tell me this small thing, yet are bold to name a large one — telling us what is in the stomach of the unborn morrow: that we shall not have those men. Now it is my thought that they will be with us."

That made a stir. All wanted to know why she thought that. But La Hire took the word and said:

"Let be. If she thinks it, that is enough. It will happen."

Then Pothon of Saintrailles said:

"There were other reasons for declining battle, according to the saying of your Excellency?"

"Yes. One was that we being weak and the day far gone, the battle might not be decisive. When it is fought it *must* be decisive. And shall be."

"God grant it, and amen. There were still other reasons?"

"One other — yes." She hesitated a moment, then said: "This was not the day. To-morrow is the day. It is so written."

They were going to assail her with eager questionings, but she put up her hand and prevented them. Then she said:

"It will be the most noble and beneficent victory that God has vouchsafed to France at any time. I pray you question me not as to whence or how I know this thing, but be content that it is so."

There was pleasure in every face, and conviction and high confidence. A murmur of conversation broke out, but was interrupted by a messenger from the outposts who brought news—namely, that for an hour there had been stir and movement in the English camp of a sort unusual at such a time and with a resting army, he said. Spies had been sent under cover of the rain and darkness to inquire into it. They had just come back and reported that large bodies of men had been dimly made out who were slipping stealthily away in the direction of Meung.

The generals were very much surprised, as any might tell from their faces.

"It is a retreat," said Joan.

"It has that look," said D'Alençon.

"It certainly has," observed the Bastard and La Hire.

"It was not to be expected," said Louis de Bourbon, "but one can divine the purpose of it."

"Yes," responded Joan. "Talbot has reflected. His rash brain has cooled. He thinks to take the bridge of Meung and escape to the other side of the river. He knows that this leaves his garrison of Beaugency at the mercy of fortune, to escape our hands if it can; but there is no other course if he would avoid this battle, and that he also knows. But he shall not get the bridge. We will see to that."

"Yes," said D'Alençon, "we must follow him, and take care of that matter. What of Beaugency?"

"Leave Beaugency to me, gentle duke; I will have it in two hours, and at no cost of blood."

"It is true, Excellency. You will but need to deliver this news there and receive the surrender."

"Yes. And I will be with you at Meung with the dawn, fetching the Constable and his fifteen hundred; and when Talbot knows that Beaugency has fallen it will have an effect upon him."

"By the mass, yes!" cried La Hire. "He will join his Meung garrison to his army and break for Paris. Then we shall have our bridge force with us again, along with our Beaugency-watchers, and be stronger for our great day's work by four-and-twenty hundred able soldiers, as was here promised within the hour. Verily this Englishman is doing our errands for us and saving us much blood and trouble. Orders, Excellency — give us our orders!"

"They are simple. Let the men rest three hours longer. At one o'clock the advance-guard will march, under your command, with Pothon of Saintrailles as second; the second division will follow at two under the Lieutenant-General. Keep well in the rear of the enemy, and see to it that you avoid an engagement. I will ride under guard to Beaugency and make so quick work there that I and the Constable of France will join you before dawn with his men.''

She kept her word. Her guard mounted and we rode off through the puttering rain, taking with us a captured English officer to confirm Joan's news. We soon covered the journey and summoned the castle. Richard Guétin, Talbot's lieutenant, being convinced that he and his five hundred men were left helpless, conceded that it would be useless to try to hold out. He could not expect easy terms, yet Joan granted them nevertheless. His garrison could keep their horses and arms, and carry away property to the value of a silver mark per man. They could go whither they pleased, but must not take arms against France again under ten days.

Before dawn we were with our army again, and with us the Constable and nearly all his men, for we left only a small garrison in Beaugency castle. We heard the dull booming of cannon to the front, and knew that Talbot was beginning his attack on the bridge. But some time before it was yet light the sound ceased and we heard it no more.

Guétin had sent a messenger through our lines under a safe-conduct given by Joan, to tell Talbot of the surrender. Of course this poursuivant had arrived ahead of us. Talbot had held it wisdom to turn now and retreat upon Paris. When daylight came he had disappeared; and with him Lord Scales and the garrison of Meung.

What a harvest of English strongholds we had reaped in those three days! — strongholds which had defied France with quite cool confidence and plenty of it until we came.

CHAPTER XXX.

WHEN the morning broke at last on that forever memorable 18th of June, there was no enemy discoverable anywhere, as I have said. But that did not trouble me. I knew we should find him, and that we should strike him; strike him the promised blow — the one from which the English power in France would not rise up in a thousand years, as Joan had said in her trance.

The enemy had plunged into the wide plains of La Beauce — a roadless waste covered with bushes, with here and there bodies of forest trees — a region where an army would be hidden from view in a very little while. We found the trail in the soft wet earth and followed it. It indicated an orderly march; no confusion, no panic.

But we had to be cautious. In such a piece of country we could walk into an ambush without any trouble. Therefore Joan sent bodies of cavalry ahead under La Hire, Pothon, and other captains, to feel the way. Some of the other officers began to show uneasiness; this sort of hide-and-go-seek business troubled them and made their confidence a little shaky. Joan divined their state of mind and cried out impetuously:

"Name of God, what would you? We must smite these English, and we will. They shall not escape us. Though they were hung to the clouds we would get them!"

By and by we were nearing Patay; it was about a league away. Now at this time our reconnoissance, feeling its way in the bush, frightened a deer, and it went bounding away and was out of sight in a moment. Then hardly a minute later a dull great shout went up in the distance toward Patay. It was the English soldiery. They had been shut up in garrison so long on mouldy food that they could not keep their delight to themselves when this fine fresh meat came springing into their midst. Poor creature, it had wrought damage to a nation which loved it well. For the French knew where the English were now, whereas the English had no suspicion of where the French were.

La Hire halted where he was, and sent back the tidings. Joan was radiant with joy. The Duke d'Alençon said to her:

"Very well, we have found them; shall we fight them?"

"Have you good spurs, prince?"

"Why? Will they make us run away?"

"Nenni, en nom de Dieu! These English are ours — they are lost. They will fly. Who overtakes them will need good spurs. Forward—close up!"

By the time we had come up with La Hire the English had discovered our presence. Talbot's force was marching in three bodies. First his advance-guard; then his artillery; then his battle corps a good way in the rear. He was now out of the bush and in a fair open country. He at once posted his artillery, his advance-guard, and five hundred picked archers along some hedges where the French would be obliged to pass, and hoped to hold this position till his battle corps could come up. Sir John Fastolfe urged the battle corps into a gallop. Joan saw her opportunity and ordered La Hire to advance—which La Hire promptly did, launching his wild riders like a storm-wind, his customary fashion.

The Duke and the Bastard wanted to follow, but Joan said:

"Not yet—wait."

So they waited—impatiently, and fidgeting in their saddles. But she was steady—gazing straight before her, measuring, weighing, calculating—by shades, minutes, fractions of minutes, seconds—with all her great soul present, in eye, and set of head, and noble pose of body—but patient, steady, master of herself—master of herself and of the situation.

And yonder, receding, receding, plumes lifting and falling, lifting and falling, streamed the thundering charge of La Hire's godless crew, La Hire's great figure dominating it and his sword stretched aloft like a flagstaff.

"Oh, Satan and his Hellions, see them go!" Somebody muttered it in deep admiration.

And now he was closing up—closing up on Fastolfe's rushing corps.

And now he struck it—struck it hard, and broke its order. It lifted the duke and the Bastard in their saddles to see it; and they turned, trembling with excitement, to Joan, saying:

"*Now!*"

But she put up her hand, still gazing, weighing, calculating, and said again:

"Wait—not yet."

Fastolfe's hard-driven battle corps raged on like an avalanche toward the waiting advance-guard. Suddenly these conceived the idea that it was flying in panic before Joan; and so in that instant it broke and swarmed away in a mad panic itself, with Talbot storming and cursing after it.

Now was the golden time. Joan drove her spurs home and waved the advance with her sword. "Follow me!" she cried, and bent her head to her horse's neck and sped away like the wind!

We swept down into the confusion of that flying rout, and for three long hours we cut and hacked and stabbed. At last the bugles sang "Halt!"

The Battle of Patay was won.

Joan of Arc dismounted, and stood surveying

that awful field, lost in thought. Presently she said:

"The praise is to God. He has smitten with a heavy hand this day." After a little she lifted her face, and looking afar off, said, with the manner of one who is thinking aloud, "In a thousand years — a thousand years — the English power in France will not rise up from this blow." She stood again a time thinking, then she turned toward her grouped generals, and there was a glory in her face and a noble light in her eye; and she said:

"Oh, friends, friends, do you know? — do you comprehend? *France is on the way to be free!*"

"And had never been, but for Joan of Arc!" said La Hire, passing before her and bowing low, the others following and doing likewise; he muttering as he went, "I will say it though I be damned for it." Then battalion after battalion of our victorious army swung by, wildly cheering. And they shouted "Live forever, Maid of Orleans, live forever!" while Joan, smiling, stood at the salute with her sword.

This was not the last time I saw the Maid of Orleans on the red field of Patay. Toward the end of the day I came upon her where the dead and dying lay stretched all about in heaps and winrows; our men had mortally wounded an English prisoner who was too poor to pay a ransom, and from a distance she had seen that cruel thing done; and had galloped to the place and sent for a priest, and now

JOAN AND THE WOUNDED ENGLISH SOLDIER

she was holding the head of her dying enemy in her lap, and easing him to his death with comforting soft words, just as his sister might have done; and the womanly tears running down her face all the time.*

* Lord Ronald Gower (*Joan of Arc*, p. 82) says: "Michelet discovered this story in the deposition of Joan of Arc's page, Louis de Conte, who was probably an eyewitness of the scene." This is true. It was a part of the testimony of the author of these "Personal Recollections of Joan of Arc," given by him in the Rehabilitation proceedings of 1456.—TRANSLATOR.

CHAPTER XXXI.

JOAN had said true: France was on the way to be free.

The war called the Hundred Years' War was very sick to-day. Sick on its English side—for the very first time since its birth, ninety-one years gone by.

Shall we judge battles by the numbers killed and the ruin wrought? Or shall we not rather judge them by the results which flowed from them? Any one will say that a battle is only truly great or small according to its results. Yes, any one will grant that, for it is the truth.

Judged by results, Patay's place is with the few supremely great and imposing battles that have been fought since the peoples of the world first resorted to arms for the settlement of their quarrels. So judged, it is even possible that Patay has no peer among that few just mentioned, but stands alone, as the supremest of historic conflicts. For when it began France lay gasping out the remnant of an exhausted life, her case wholly hopeless in the view of all political physicians; when it ended, three hours later, she was convalescent. Convalescent, and nothing requisite but time and ordinary nursing to bring her back to perfect health. The dullest physician of them all could see this, and there was none to deny it.

Many death-sick nations have reached convalescence through a series of battles, a procession of battles, a weary tale of wasting conflicts stretching over years, but only one has reached it in a single day and by a single battle. That nation is France, and that battle Patay.

Remember it and be proud of it; for you are French, and it is the stateliest fact in the long annals of your country. There it stands, with its head in the clouds! And when you grow up you will go on pilgrimage to the field of Patay, and stand uncovered in the presence of — what? A monument with *its* head in the clouds? Yes. For all nations in all times have built monuments on their battlefields to keep green the memory of the perishable deed that was wrought there and of the perishable name of him who wrought it; and will France neglect Patay and Joan of Arc? Not for long. And will she build a monument scaled to their rank as compared with the world's other fields and heroes? Perhaps — if there be room for it under the arch of the sky.

But let us look back a little, and consider certain strange and impressive facts. The Hundred Years' War began in 1337. It raged on and on, year after year and year after year; and at last England stretched France prone with that fearful blow at

Crécy. But she rose and struggled on, year after year, and at last again she went down under another devastating blow — Poitiers. She gathered her crippled strength once more, and the war raged on, and on, and still on, year after year, decade after decade. Children were born, grew up, married, died — the war raged on; *their* children in turn grew up, married, died — the war raged on; *their* children, growing, saw France struck down again; this time under the incredible disaster of Agincourt — and still the war raged on, year after year, and in time *these* children married in their turn.

France was a wreck, a ruin, a desolation. The half of it belonged to England, with none to dispute or deny the truth; the other half belonged to nobody — in three months would be flying the English flag; the French King was making ready to throw away his crown and flee beyond the seas.

Now came the ignorant country maid out of her remote village and confronted this hoary war, this all-consuming conflagration that had swept the land for three generations. Then began the briefest and most amazing campaign that is recorded in history. In seven weeks it was finished. In seven weeks she hopelessly crippled that gigantic war that was ninety-one years old. At Orleans she struck it a staggering blow; on the field of Patay she broke its back.

Think of it. Yes, one can do that; but *understand* it? Ah, that is another matter; none will ever be able to comprehend that stupefying marvel.

Seven weeks — with here and there a little bloodshed. Perhaps the most of it, in any single fight, at Patay, where the English began six thousand strong and left two thousand dead upon the field. It is said and believed that in three battles alone — Crécy, Poitiers, and Agincourt — near a hundred thousand Frenchmen fell, without counting the thousand other fights of that long war. The dead of that war make a mournful long list — an interminable list. Of men slain in the field the count goes by tens of thousands; of innocent women and children slain by bitter hardship and hunger it goes by that appalling term, millions.

It was an ogre, that war; an ogre that went about for near a hundred years, crunching men and dripping blood from his jaws. And with her little hand that child of seventeen struck him down; and yonder he lies stretched on the field of Patay, and will not get up any more while this old world lasts.

CHAPTER XXXII.

THE great news of Patay was carried over the whole of France in twenty hours, people said. I do not know as to that; but one thing is sure, anyway: the moment a man got it he flew shouting and glorifying God and told his neighbor; and that neighbor flew with it to the next homestead; and so on and so on without resting the word traveled; and when a man got it in the night, at what hour soever, he jumped out of his bed and bore the blessed message along. And the joy that went with it was like the light that flows across the land when an eclipse is receding from the face of the sun; and, indeed, you may say that France had lain in an eclipse this long time; yes, buried in a black gloom which these beneficent tidings were sweeping away now before the onrush of their white splendor.

The news beat the flying enemy to Yeuville, and the town rose against its English masters and shut the gates against their brethren. It flew to Mont Pipeau, to Saint Simon, and to this, that, and the other English fortress; and straightway the garrison applied the torch and took to the fields and the woods. A detachment of our army occupied Meung and pillaged it.

When we reached Orleans that town was as much as fifty times insaner with joy than we had ever seen it before — which is saying much. Night had just fallen, and the illuminations were on so wonderful a scale that we seemed to plow through seas of fire; and as to the noise — the hoarse cheering of the multitude, the thundering of cannon, the clash of bells — indeed, there was never anything like it. And everywhere rose a new cry that burst upon us like a storm when the column entered the gates, and nevermore ceased: "Welcome to Joan of Arc — way for the SAVIOUR OF FRANCE!" And there was another cry: "Crécy is avenged! Poitiers is avenged! Agincourt is avenged! — Patay shall live forever!"

Mad? Why, you never could imagine it in the world. The prisoners were in the center of the column. When that came along and the people caught sight of their masterful old enemy Talbot, that had made them dance so long to his grim war-music, you may imagine what the uproar was like if you can, for I cannot describe it. They were so glad to see him that presently they wanted to have him out and hang him; so Joan had him brought up to the front to ride in her protection. They made a striking pair.

CHAPTER XXXIII.

YES, Orleans was in a delirium of felicity. She invited the King, and made sumptuous preparations to receive him, but—he didn't come. He was simply a serf at that time, and La Tremouille was his master. Master and serf were visiting together at the master's castle of Sully-sur-Loire.

At Beaugency Joan had engaged to bring about a reconciliation between the Constable Richemont and the King. She took Richemont to Sully-sur-Loire and made her promise good.

The great deeds of Joan of Arc are five:

1. The Raising of the Siege.
2. The Victory of Patay.
3. The Reconciliation at Sully-sur-Loire.
4. The Coronation of the King.
5. The Blôodless March.

We shall come to the Bloodless March presently (and the Coronation). It was the victorious long march which Joan made through the enemy's country from Gien to Rheims, and thence to the gates of Paris, capturing every English town and fortress that barred the road, from the beginning of the journey to the end of it; and this by the mere force of her name, and without shedding a drop of blood — perhaps the most extraordinary campaign in this regard in history — this is the most glorious of her military exploits.

The Reconciliation was one of Joan's most important achievements. No one else could have accomplished it; and, in fact, no one else of high consequence had any disposition to try. In brains, in scientific warfare, and in statesmanship the Constable Richemont was the ablest man in France. His loyalty was sincere; his probity was above suspicion — (and it made him sufficiently conspicuous in that trivial and conscienceless Court).

In restoring Richemont to France, Joan made thoroughly secure the successful completion of the great work which she had begun. She had never seen Richemont until he came to her with his little army. Was it not wonderful that at a glance she should know him for the one man who could finish and perfect her work and establish it in perpetuity? How was it that that child was able to do this? It was because she had the "seeing eye," as one of our knights had once said. Yes, she had that great gift — almost the highest and rarest that has been granted to man. Nothing of an extraordinary sort was still to be done, yet the remaining work could not safely be left to the King's idiots; for it would require wise statesmanship and long and patient though desultory hammering of the enemy. Now and then, for a quarter of a century yet, there would be a little fighting to do, and a handy man could carry that on with small disturbance to the rest of the country; and little by little, and with progressive certainty, the English would disappear from France.

And that happened. Under the influence of Richemont the King became at a later time a man — a man, a king, a brave and capable and determined soldier. Within six years after Patay he was leading storming parties himself; fighting in fortress ditches up to his waist in water, and climbing scaling-ladders under a furious fire with a pluck that would have satisfied even Joan of Arc. In time he and Richemont cleared away all the English; even from regions where the people had been under their mastership for three hundred years. In such regions wise and careful work was necessary, for the English rule had been fair and kindly; and men who have been ruled in that way are not always anxious for a change.

Which of Joan's five chief deeds shall we call chiefest? It is my thought that each *in its turn* was that. This is saying that, taken as a whole, they *equalized* each other, and neither was then greater than its mate.

Do you perceive? Each was a stage in an ascent. To leave out one of them would defeat the journey; to achieve one of them at the wrong time and in the wrong place would have the same effect.

Consider the Coronation. As a masterpiece of diplomacy, where can you find its superior in our history? Did the King suspect its vast importance? No. Did his ministers? No. Did the astute Bedford, representative of the English crown? No. An advantage of incalculable importance was here under the eyes of the King and of Bedford; the King could get it by a bold stroke, Bedford could get it without an effort; but, being ignorant of its value, neither of them put forth his hand. Of all the wise people in high office in France, only one knew the priceless worth of this neglected prize — the untaught child of seventeen, Joan of Arc — and she had known it from the beginning, had spoken of it from the beginning as an essential detail of her mission.

How did she know it? It is simple: she was a peasant. That tells the whole story. She was of the people and knew the people; those others moved in a loftier sphere and knew nothing much about them. We make little account of that vague, formless, inert mass, that mighty underlying force which we call "the people" — an epithet which carries contempt with it. It is a strange attitude; for at bottom we know that the throne which the people support stands, and that when that support is removed nothing in this world can save it.

Now, then, consider this fact, and observe its importance. Whatever the parish priest believes his flock believes; they love him, they revere him; he is their unfailing friend, their dauntless protector, their comforter in sorrow, their helper in their day of need; he has their whole confidence; what he tells them to do, that they will do, with a blind and affectionate obedience, let it cost what it may. Add these facts thoughtfully together, and what is the sum? This: *The parish priest governs the nation.* What is the King, then, if the parish priest withdraw his support and deny his authority? Merely a shadow and no King; let him resign.

Do you get that idea? Then let us proceed. A priest is consecrated to his office by the awful hand of God, laid upon him by his appointed representative on earth. That consecration is final; nothing can undo it, nothing can remove it. Neither the Pope nor any other power can strip the priest of his office; God gave it, and it is forever sacred and secure. The dull parish knows all this. To priest and parish, whosoever is anointed of God bears an office whose authority can no longer be disputed or assailed. To the parish priest, and to his subjects the nation, an uncrowned king is a similitude of a person who has been named for holy orders but has not been consecrated; he has no office, he has not been ordained, another may be appointed in his place. In a word, an uncrowned king is a *doubtful* king; but if God appoint him and His servant the Bishop anoint him, the doubt is annihilated; the priest and the parish are his loyal subjects straightway, and while he lives they will recognize no king but him.

To Joan of Arc the peasant girl, Charles VII. was no King until he was crowned; to her he was only the *Dauphin;* that is to say, the *heir.* If I have ever made her call him King, it was a mistake; she called him the Dauphin, and nothing else until after the Coronation. It shows you as in a mirror — for Joan was a mirror in which the lowly hosts of France were clearly reflected — that to all that vast underlying force called "the people" he was no King but only Dauphin before his crowning, and was indisputably and irrevocably King *after* it.

Now you understand what a colossal move on the political chessboard the Coronation was. Bedford realized this by and by, and tried to patch up his mistake by crowning *his* King; but what good could that do? None in the world.

Speaking of chess, Joan's great acts may be likened to that game. Each move was made in its proper order, and it was great and effective because it *was* made in its proper order and not out of it. Each, at the time made, seemed the greatest move; but the final result made them all recognizable as equally essential and equally important. This is the game, as played:

1. Joan moves Orleans and Patay — *check.*

2. Then moves the Reconciliation — but does not proclaim check, it being a move for position, and to take effect later.

3. Next she moves the Coronation—*check.*

4. Next, the Bloodless March—*check.*

5. Final move (after her death) the reconciled Constable Richemont to the French King's elbow—*checkmate.*

CHAPTER XXXIV.

THE Campaign of the Loire had as good as opened the road to Rheims. There was no sufficient reason now why the Coronation should not take place. The Coronation would complete the mission which Joan had received from heaven, and then she would be forever done with war, and would fly home to her mother and her sheep, and never stir from the hearthstone and happiness any more. That was her dream; and she could not rest, she was so impatient to see it fulfilled. She became so possessed with this matter that I began to lose faith in her two prophecies of her early death — and, of course, when I found that faith wavering I encouraged it to waver all the more.

The King was afraid to start to Rheims, because the road was mile-posted with English fortresses, so to speak. Joan held them in light esteem and not things to be afraid of in the existing modified condition of English confidence.

And she was right. As it turned out, the march to Rheims was nothing but a holiday excursion, Joan did not even take any artillery along, she was so sure it would not be necessary. We marched from Gien twelve thousand strong. This was the 29th of June. The Maid rode by the side of the King; on his other side was the Duke d'Alençon. After the duke followed three other princes of the blood. After these followed the Bastard of Orleans, the Marshal de Boussac, and the Admiral of France. After these came La Hire, Saintrailles, Tremouille, and a long procession of knights and nobles.

We rested three days before Auxerre. The city provisioned the army, and a deputation waited upon the King, but we did not enter the place.

Saint-Florentin opened its gates to the King.

On the 4th of July we reached Saint-Fal, and yonder lay Troyes before us — a town which had a burning interest for us boys; for we remembered how seven years before, in the pastures of Domremy, the Sunflower came with his black flag and brought us the shameful news of the Treaty of Troyes — that treaty which gave France to England, and a daughter of our royal line in marriage to the Butcher of Agincourt. That poor town was not to blame, of course; yet we flushed hot with that old memory, and hoped there would be a misunderstanding here, for we dearly wanted to storm the place and burn it. It was powerfully garrisoned by English and Burgundian soldiery, and was expecting re-enforcements from Paris. Before night we camped before its gates and made rough work with a sortie which marched out against us.

Joan summoned Troyes to surrender. Its commandant, seeing that she had no artillery, scoffed at the idea, and sent her a grossly insulting reply. Five days we consulted and negotiated. No result. The King was about to turn back now and give up. He was afraid to go on, leaving this strong place in his rear. Then La Hire put in a word, with a slap in it for some of his Majesty's advisers:

"The Maid of Orleans undertook this expedition of her own motion; and it is my mind that it is her judgment that should be followed here, and not that of any other, let him be of whatsoever breed and standing he may."

There was wisdom and righteousness in that. So the King sent for the Maid, and asked her how she thought the prospect looked. She said, without any tone of doubt or question in her voice:

"In three days' time the place is ours."

The smug Chancellor put in a word now:

"If we were sure of it we would wait here six days."

"Six days, forsooth! Name of God, man, we will enter the gates to-morrow!"

Then she mounted, and rode her lines, crying out:

"Make preparation — to your work, friends, to your work! We assault at dawn!"

She worked hard that night; slaving away with her own hands like a common soldier. She ordered fascines and fagots to be prepared and thrown into the fosse, thereby to bridge it; and in this rough labor she took a man's share.

At dawn she took her place at the head of the storming force and the bugles blew the assault. At that moment a flag of truce was flung to the breeze from the walls, and Troyes surrendered without firing a shot.

The next day the King with Joan at his side and the Paladin bearing her banner entered the town in state at the head of the army. And a goodly army it was now, for it had been growing ever bigger and bigger from the first.

And now a curious thing happened. By the terms of the treaty made with the town the garrison of English and Burgundian soldiery were to be allowed to carry away their "goods" with them. This was well, for otherwise how would they buy the wherewithal to live? Very well; these people were all to go out by the one gate, and at the time set for them to depart we young fellows went to that gate, along with the Dwarf, to see the march-out. Presently here they came in an interminable file, the foot-soldiers in the lead. As they approached one could see that each bore a burden of a bulk and weight to sorely tax his strength; and we said among ourselves, truly these folk are well off for poor common soldiers. When they were come nearer, what do you think? Every rascal of them had a French prisoner on his back! They were carrying away their "goods," you see — their property — strictly according to the permission granted by the treaty.

Now think how clever that was, how ingenious. What could a body say? what could a body do? For certainly these people were within their right. These prisoners were property; nobody could deny that. My dears, if those had been *English* captives, conceive of the richness of that booty! For English prisoners had been scarce and precious for a hundred years; whereas it was a different matter with French prisoners. They had been overabundant for a century. The possessor of a French prisoner did not hold him long for ransom, as a rule, but presently killed him to save the cost of his keep. This shows you how small was the value of such a possession in those times. When we took Troyes a calf was worth thirty francs, a sheep sixteen, a French prisoner eight. It was an enormous price for those other animals — a price which naturally seems incredible to you. It was the war, you see. It worked two ways: it made meat dear and prisoners cheap.

Well, here were these poor Frenchmen being carried off. What could we do? Very little of a permanent sort, but we did what we could. We sent a messenger flying to Joan, and we and the French guards halted the procession for a parley — to gain time, you see. A big Burgundian lost his temper and swore a great oath that none should stop *him;* he would go, and would take his prisoner with him. But we blocked him off, and he saw that he was mistaken about going — he couldn't do it. He exploded into the maddest cursings and revilings, then, and, unlashing his prisoner from his back, stood him up, all bound and helpless; then drew his knife, and said to us with a light of sarcastic triumph in his eye:

"I may not carry him away, you say—yet he is mine, none will dispute it. Since I may not convey him hence, this property of mine, there is another way. Yes, I can kill him; not even the dullest among you will question *that* right. Ah, you had not thought of that—vermin!"

That poor starved fellow begged us with his piteous eyes to save him; then spoke, and said he had a wife and little children at home. Think how it wrung our heartstrings. But what could we do? The Burgundian was within his right. We could only beg and plead for the prisoner. Which we did. And the Burgundian enjoyed it. He stayed his hand to hear more of it, and laugh at it. That stung. Then the Dwarf said:

"Prithee, young sirs, let me beguile him; for when a matter requiring persuasion is to the fore, I have indeed a gift in that sort, as any will tell you that know me well. You smile; and that is punishment for my vanity, and fairly earned, I grant it you. Still, if I may toy a little, just a little—" saying which he stepped to the Burgundian and began a fair soft speech, all of goodly and gentle tenor; and in the midst he mentioned the Maid; and was going on to say how she out of her good heart would prize and praise this compassionate deed which he was about to —

It was as far as he got. The Burgundian burst into his smooth oration with an insult leveled at Joan of Arc. We sprang forward, but the Dwarf, his face all livid, brushed us aside and said, in a most grave and earnest way:

"I crave your patience. Am not I her guard of honor? This is my affair."

And saying this he suddenly shot his right hand out and gripped the great Burgundian by the throat, and so held him upright on his feet. "You have insulted the Maid," he said; "and the Maid is France. The tongue that does that earns a long furlough."

One heard the muffled cracking of bones. The Burgundian's eyes began to protrude from their sockets and stare with a leaden dullness at vacancy. The color deepened in his face and became an opaque purple. His hands hung down limp, his body collapsed with a shiver, every muscle relaxed its tension and ceased from its function. The Dwarf took away his hand and the column of inert mortality sank mushily to the ground.

We struck the bonds from the prisoner and told him he was free. His crawling humbleness changed to frantic joy in a moment, and his ghastly fear to a childish rage. He flew at that dead corpse and kicked it, spat in its face, danced upon it, crammed mud into its mouth, laughing, jeering, cursing, and volleying forth indecencies and bestialities like a drunken fiend. It was a thing to be expected: soldiering makes few saints. Many of the onlookers laughed, others were indifferent, none was surprised. But presently in his mad caperings the freed man capered within reach of the waiting file, and another Burgundian promptly slipped a knife through his neck, and down he went with a death-shriek, his brilliant artery-blood spurting ten feet as straight and bright as a ray of light. There was a great burst of jolly laughter all around from friend and foe alike; and thus closed one of the pleasantest incidents of my checkered military life.

And now came Joan hurrying, and deeply troubled. She considered the claim of the garrison, then said:

"You have right upon your side. It is plain. It was a careless word to put in the treaty, and covers too much. But ye may not take these poor men away. They are French, and I will not have it. The King shall ransom them, every one. Wait till I send you word from him; and hurt no hair of their heads; for I tell you, I who speak, that that would cost you very dear."

That settled it. The prisoners were safe for one while, anyway. Then she rode back eagerly and required that thing of the King, and would listen to no paltering and no excuses. So the King told her to have her way, and she rode straight back and bought the captives free in his name and let them go.

CHAPTER XXXV.

IT was here that we saw again the Grand Master of the King's Household, in whose castle Joan was guest when she tarried at Chinon in those first days of her coming out of her own country. She made him Bailiff of Troyes now by the King's permission.

And now we marched again; Châlons surrendered to us; and there by Châlons in a talk, Joan, being asked if she had no fears for the future, said yes, one—treachery. Who could believe it? who could dream it? And yet in a sense it was prophecy. Truly, man is a pitiful animal.

We marched, marched, kept on marching; and at last, on the 16th of July, we came in sight of our goal, and saw the great cathedral towers of Rheims rise out of the distance! Huzza after huzza swept the army from van to rear; and as for Joan of Arc, there where she sat her horse gazing, clothed all in white armor, dreamy, beautiful, and in her face a deep, deep joy, a joy not of earth, oh, she was not flesh, she was a spirit! Her sublime mission was closing—closing in flawless triumph. To-morrow she could say, "It is finished — let me go free."

We camped, and the hurry and rush and turmoil of the grand preparations began. The Archbishop and a great deputation arrived; and after these came flock after flock, crowd after crowd, of citizens and country folk, hurrahing, in, with banners and music, and flowed over the camp, one rejoicing inundation after another, everybody drunk with happiness. And all night long Rheims was hard at work, hammering away, decorating the town, building triumphal arches and clothing the ancient cathedral within and without in a glory of opulent splendors.

We moved betimes in the morning; the coronation ceremonies would begin at nine and last five hours. We were aware that the garrison of English and Burgundian soldiers had given up all thought of resisting the Maid, and that we should find the gates standing hospitably open and the whole city ready to welcome us with enthusiasm.

It was a delicious morning, brilliant with sunshine, but cool and fresh and inspiring. The army was in great form, and fine to see, as it uncoiled from its lair fold by fold, and stretched away on the final march of the peaceful Coronation Campaign.

Joan, on her black horse, with the Lieutenant-General and the personal staff grouped about her, took post for a final review and a good-bye; for she was not expecting to ever be a soldier again, or ever serve with these or any other soldiers any more after this day. The army knew this, and believed it was looking for the last time upon the girlish face of its invincible little Chief, its pet, its pride, its darling, whom it had ennobled in its private heart with nobilities of its own creation, calling her "Daughter of God," "Saviour of France," "Victory's Sweetheart," "the Page of Christ," together with still softer titles which were simply naïf and frank endearments such as men are used to confer upon children whom they love. And so one saw a new thing now; a thing bred of the emotion that was present there on both sides. Always before, in the march-past, the battalions had gone swinging by in a storm of cheers, heads up and eyes flashing, the drums rolling, the bands braying pæans of victory; but now there was nothing of that. But for one impressive sound, one could have closed his eyes and imagined himself in a world of the dead. That one sound was all that visited the ear in the summer stillness—just that one sound—the muffled tread of the marching host. As the serried masses drifted by, the men put their right hands up to their temples, palms to the front, in military salute, turning their eyes upon Joan's face in mute God-bless-you and farewell, and keeping them there while they could. They still kept their hands up in reverent salute many steps after they had passed by. Every time Joan put her handkerchief to her eyes you could see a little quiver of emotion crinkle along the faces of the files.

The march-past after a victory is a thing to drive the heart mad with jubilation; but this one was a thing to break it.

We rode now to the King's lodging, which was the Archbishop's country palace; and he was presently ready, and we galloped off and took position at the head of the army. By this time the country people were arriving in multitudes from every direction and massing themselves on both sides of the road to get sight of Joan — just as had been done every day since our first day's march began. Our march now lay through the grassy plain, and those peasants made a dividing double border for that plain. They stretched right down through it, a broad belt of bright colors on each side of the road; for every peasant girl and woman in it had a white jacket on her body and a crimson skirt on the rest of her. Endless borders made of poppies and lilies stretching away in front of us — that is what it looked like. And that is the kind of lane we had been marching through all these days. Not a lane between multitudinous flowers standing upright on their stems — no, these flowers were always kneeling; kneeling, these human flowers, with their hands and faces lifted toward Joan of Arc, and the grateful tears streaming down. And all along, those closest to the road hugged her feet and kissed them and laid their wet cheeks fondly against them. I never, during all those days, saw any of either sex stand while she passed, nor any man keep his head covered. Afterwards in the Great Trial these touching scenes were used as a weapon against her. She had been made an object of adoration by the people, and this was proof that she was a heretic — so claimed that unjust court.

As we drew near the city the curving long sweep of ramparts and towers was gay with fluttering flags and black with masses of people; and all the air was vibrant with the crash of artillery and gloomed with drifting clouds of smoke. We entered the gates in state and moved in procession through the city, with all the guilds and industries in holiday costume marching in our rear with their banners; and all the route was hedged with a huzzaing crush of people, and all the windows were full and all the roofs; and from the balconies hung costly stuffs of rich colors; and the waving of handkerchiefs, seen in perspective through a long vista, was like a snow-storm.

Joan's name had been introduced into the prayers of the Church — an honor theretofore restricted to royalty. But she had a dearer honor and an honor more to be proud of, from a humbler source: the common people had had leaden medals struck which bore her effigy and her escutcheon, and these they wore as charms. One saw them everywhere.

From the Archbishop's Palace, where we halted, and where the King and Joan were to lodge, the King sent to the Abbey Church of St. Remi, which was over toward the gate by which we had entered the city, for the *Sainte Ampoule*, or flask of holy oil. This oil was not earthly oil; it was made in heaven; the flask also. The flask, with the oil in it, was brought down from heaven by a dove. It was sent down to St. Remi just as he was going to baptize King Clovis, who had become a Christian. I know this to be true. I had known it long before; for Père Fronte told me in Domremy. I cannot tell you how strange and awful it made me feel when I saw that flask and knew I was looking with my own eyes upon a thing which had actually been in heaven; a thing which had been seen by angels, perhaps; and by God Himself of a certainty, for He sent it. And I was looking upon it — I. At one time I could have touched it. But I was afraid; for I could not know but that God had touched it. It is most probable that He had.

From this flask Clovis had been anointed; and from it all the kings of France had been anointed since. Yes, ever since the time of Clovis; and that was nine hundred years. And so, as I have said, that flask of holy oil was sent for, while we waited. A coronation without that would not have been a coronation at all, in my belief.

Now in order to get the flask, a most ancient ceremonial had to be gone through with; otherwise the Abbé of St. Remi, hereditary guardian in perpetuity of the oil, would not deliver it. So, in accordance with custom, the King deputed five great nobles to ride in solemn state and richly armed and accoutered, they and their steeds, to the Abbey Church as a guard of honor to the Archbishop of Rheims and his canons, who were to bear the King's demand for the oil. When the five great lords were ready to start, they knelt in a row and put up their mailed hands before their faces, palm joined to palm, and swore upon their lives to conduct the sacred vessel safely, and safely restore it again to the Church of St. Remi after the anointing of the King. The Archbishop and his subordinates, thus nobly escorted, took their way to St. Remi. The Archbishop was in grand costume, with his mitre on his head and his cross in his hand. At the door of St. Remi they halted and formed, to receive the holy phial. Soon one heard the deep tones of the organ and of chanting men; then one saw a long file of lights approaching through the dim church. And so came the Abbot, in his sacerdotal panoply, bearing the phial, with his people following after. He delivered it, with solemn ceremonies, to the Archbishop; then the march back began, and it was most impressive; for it moved, the whole way, between two multitudes of men and women who lay flat upon their faces and prayed in dumb silence and in dread while that awful thing went by that had been in heaven.

This august company arrived at the great west door of the cathedral; and as the Archbishop entered a noble anthem rose and filled the vast building. The cathedral was packed with people —

people in thousands. Only a wide space down the center had been kept free. Down this space walked the Archbishop and his canons, and after them followed those five stately figures in splendid harness, each bearing his feudal banner—and riding!

Oh, that was a magnificent thing to see. Riding down the cavernous vastness of the building through the rich lights streaming in long rays from the pictured windows—oh, there was never anything so grand!

They rode clear to the choir—as much as four hundred feet from the door, it was said. Then the Archbishop dismissed them, and they made deep obeisance till their plumes touched their horses' necks, then made those proud prancing and mincing and dancing creatures go backwards all the way to the door—which was pretty to see, and graceful; then they stood them on their hind-feet and spun them around and plunged away and disappeared.

For some minutes there was a deep hush, a waiting pause; a silence so profound that it was as if all those packed thousands there were steeped in dreamless slumber—why, you could even notice the faintest sounds, like the drowsy buzzing of insects; then came a mighty flood of rich strains from four hundred silver trumpets, and then, framed in the pointed archway of the great west door, appeared Joan and the King. They advanced slowly, side by side, through a tempest of welcome—explosion after explosion of cheers and cries, mingled with the deep thunders of the organ and rolling tides of triumphant song from chanting choirs. Behind Joan and the King came the Paladin with the Banner displayed; and a majestic figure he was, and most proud and lofty in his bearing, for he knew that the people were marking him and taking note of the gorgeous state dress which covered his armor.

At his side was the Sire d'Albret, proxy for the Constable of France, bearing the Sword of State.

After these, in order of rank, came a body royally attired representing the lay peers of France; it consisted of three princes of the blood, and La Tremouille and the young De Laval brothers.

These were followed by the representatives of the ecclesiastical peers — the Archbishop of Rheims, and the Bishops of Laon, Châlons, Orleans, and one other.

Behind these came the Grand Staff, all our great generals and famous names, and everybody was eager to get a sight of them. Through all the din one could hear shouts all along that told you where two of them were: "Live the Bastard of Orleans!" "Satan La Hire forever!"

The august procession reached its appointed place in time, and the solemnities of the Coronation began. They were long and imposing — with prayers, and anthems, and sermons, and everything that is right for such occasions; and Joan was at the King's side all these hours, with her Standard in her hand. But at last came the grand act: the King took the oath, he was anointed with the sacred oil; a splendid personage, followed by train-bearers and other attendants, approached, bearing the Crown of France upon a cushion, and kneeling offered it. The King seemed to hesitate — in fact, *did* hesitate; for he put out his hand and then stopped with it there in the air over the crown, the fingers in the attitude of taking hold of it. But that was for only a moment — though a moment is a notable something when it stops the heart-beat of twenty thousand people and makes them catch their breath. Yes, only a moment; then he caught Joan's eye, and she gave him a look with all the joy of her thankful great soul in it, then he smiled, and took the Crown of France in his hand, and right finely and right royally lifted it up and set it upon his head.

Then what a crash there was! All about us cries and cheers, and the chanting of the choirs and groaning of the organ; and outside the clamoring of the bells and the booming of the cannon.

The fantastic dream, the incredible dream, the impossible dream of the peasant child stood fulfilled: the English power was broken, the Heir of France was crowned.

She was like one transfigured, so divine was the joy that shone in her face as she sank to her knees at the King's feet and looked up at him through her tears. Her lips were quivering, and her words came soft and low and broken:

"Now, O gentle King, is the pleasure of God

accomplished according to his command that you should come to Rheims and receive the crown that belongeth of right to you, and unto none other. My work which was given me to do is finished; give me your peace, and let me go back to my mother, who is poor and old, and has need of me."

The King raised her up, and there before all that host he praised her great deeds in most noble terms; and there he confirmed her nobility and titles, making her the equal of a count in rank, and also appointed a household and officers for her according to her dignity; and then he said:

"You have saved the crown. Speak—require—demand; and whatsoever grace you ask it shall be granted, though it make the kingdom poor to meet it."

Now that was fine, that was royal. Joan was on her knees again straightway, and said:

"Then, O gentle King, if out of your compassion you will speak the word, I pray you give commandment that my village, poor and hard pressed by reason of the war, may have its taxes remitted."

"It is so commanded. Say on."

"That is all."

"All? Nothing but that?"

"It is all. I have no other desire."

"But that is nothing—less than nothing. Ask—do not be afraid."

"Indeed, I cannot, gentle King. Do not press

me. I will not have aught else, but only this alone."

The King seemed nonplussed, and stood still a moment, as if trying to comprehend and realize the full stature of this strange unselfishness. Then he raised his head and said:

"She has won a kingdom and crowned its King; and all she asks and all she will take is this poor grace—and even this is for others, not for herself. And it is well; her act being proportioned to the dignity of one who carries in her head and heart riches which outvalue any that any King could add, though he gave his all. She shall have her way. Now, therefore, it is decreed that from this day forth Domremy, natal village of Joan of Arc, Deliverer of France, called the Maid of Orleans, is freed from all taxation *forever.*" Whereat the silver horns blew a jubilant blast.

There, you see, she had had a vision of this very scene the time she was in a trance in the pastures of Domremy, and we asked her to name the boon she would demand of the King if he should ever chance to tell her she might claim one. But whether she had the vision or not, this act showed that after all the dizzy grandeurs that had come upon her, she was still the same simple, unselfish creature that she was that day.

Yes, Charles VII. remitted those taxes "forever." Often the gratitude of kings and nations fades and their promises are forgotten or deliberately violated;

but you, who are children of France, should remember with pride that France has kept this one faithfully. Sixty-three years have gone by since that day. The taxes of the region wherein Domremy lies have been collected sixty-three times since then, and all the villages of that region have paid except that one — Domremy. The tax-gatherer never visits Domremy. Domremy has long ago forgotten what that dreaded sorrow-sowing apparition is like. Sixty-three tax-books have been filled meantime, and they lie yonder with the other public records, and any may see them that desire it. At the top of every page in the sixty-three books stands the name of a village, and below that name its weary burden of taxation is figured out and displayed; in the case of all save one. It is true, just as I tell you. In each of the sixty-three books there is a page headed "Domremi," but under that name not a figure appears. Where the figures should be, there are three words written; and the same words have been written every year for all these years; yes, it is a blank page, with always those grateful words lettered across the face of it — a touching memorial. Thus:

DOMREMI

RIEN — LA PUCELLE

"NOTHING—THE MAID OF ORLEANS." How brief it is; yet how much it says! It is the nation speaking. You have the spectacle of that unsentimental thing, a Government, making reverence to that name and saying to its agent, "*Uncover, and pass on; it is France that commands.*" Yes, the promise has been kept; it will be kept always; "forever" was the King's word.*

At two o'clock in the afternoon the ceremonies of the Coronation came at last to an end; then the procession formed once more, with Joan and the King at its head, and took up its solemn march through the midst of the church, all instruments and all people making such clamor of rejoicing noises as was, indeed, a marvel to hear. And so ended the third of the great days of Joan's life. And how close together they stand—May 8th, June 18th, July 17th!

* It was faithfully kept during three hundred and sixty years and more; then the over-confident octogenarian's prophecy failed. During the tumult of the French Revolution the promise was forgotten and the grace withdrawn. It has remained in disuse ever since. Joan never asked to be remembered, but France has remembered her with an inextinguishable love and reverence: Joan never asked for a statue, but France has lavished them upon her; Joan never asked for a church for Domremy, but France is building one; Joan never asked for saintship, but even that is impending. Everything which Joan of Arc did not ask for has been given her, and with a noble profusion; but the one humble little thing which she did ask for and get has been taken away from her. There is something infinitely pathetic about this. France owes Domremy a hundred years of taxes, and could hardly find a citizen within her borders who would vote against the payment of the debt.—NOTE BY THE TRANSLATOR.

CHAPTER XXXVI.

WE mounted and rode, a spectacle to remember, a most noble display of rich vestments and nodding plumes, and as we moved between the banked multitudes they sank down all along abreast of us as we advanced, like grain before the reaper, and kneeling hailed with a rousing welcome the consecrated King and his companion the Deliverer of France. But by and by when we had paraded about the chief parts of the city and were come near to the end of our course, we being now approaching the Archbishop's palace, one saw on the right, hard by the inn that is called the Zebra, a strange thing—two men not kneeling but *standing!* Standing in the front rank of the kneelers; unconscious, transfixed, staring. Yes, and clothed in the coarse garb of the peasantry, these two. Two halberdiers sprang at them in a fury to teach them better manners; but just as they seized them Joan cried out "Forbear!" and slid from her saddle and flung her arms about one of those peasants, calling him by all manner of endearing names, and sobbing. For it was her father; and the other was her uncle, Laxart.

The news flew everywhere, and shouts of welcome

were raised, and in just one little moment those two despised and unknown plebeians were become famous and popular and envied, and everybody was in a fever to get sight of them and be able to say, all their lives long, that they had seen the father of Joan of Arc and the brother of her mother. How easy it was for her to do miracles like to this! She was like the sun; on whatsoever dim and humble object her rays fell, that thing was straightway drowned in glory.

All graciously the King said:

"Bring them to me."

And she brought them; she radiant with happiness and affection, they trembling and scared, with their caps in their shaking hands; and there before all the world the King gave them his hand to kiss, while the people gazed in envy and admiration; and he said to old D'Arc:

"Give God thanks for that you are father to this child, this dispenser of immortalities. You who bear a name that will still live in the mouths of men when all the race of kings has been forgotten, it is not meet that you bare your head before the fleeting fames and dignities of a day—cover yourself!" And truly he looked right fine and princely when he said that. Then he gave order that the Bailly of Rheims be brought; and when he was come, and stood bent low and bare, the King said to him, "These two are guests of France;" and bade him use them hospitably.

I may as well say now as later, that Papa D'Arc and Laxart were stopping in that little Zebra inn, and that there they remained. Finer quarters were offered them by the Bailly, also public distinctions and brave entertainment; but they were frightened at these projects, they being only humble and ignorant peasants; so they begged off, and had peace. They could not have enjoyed such things. Poor souls, they did not even know what to do with their hands, and it took all their attention to keep from treading on them. The Bailly did the best he could in the circumstances. He made the innkeeper place a whole floor at their disposal, and told him to provide everything they might desire, and charge all to the city. Also the Bailly gave them a horse apiece and furnishings; which so overwhelmed them with pride and delight and astonishment that they couldn't speak a word; for in their lives they had never dreamed of wealth like this, and could not believe, at first, that the horses were real and would not dissolve to a mist and blow away. They could not unglue their minds from those grandeurs, and were always wrenching the conversation out of its groove and dragging the matter of animals into it, so that they could say "my horse" here, and "my horse" there and yonder and all around, and taste the words and lick their chops over them, and spread their legs and hitch their thumbs in their armpits, and feel as the good God feels when He looks out on His fleets of constellations plowing the awful deeps of space and reflects with satisfaction that they are His—all His. Well, they *were* the happiest old children one ever saw, and the simplest.

The city gave a grand banquet to the King and Joan in mid-afternoon, and to the Court and the Grand Staff; and about the middle of it Père d'Arc and Laxart were sent for, but would not venture until it was promised that they might sit in a gallery and be all by themselves and see all that was to be seen and yet be unmolested. And so they sat there and looked down upon the splendid spectacle, and were moved till the tears ran down their cheeks to see the unbelievable honors that were paid to their small darling, and how naïvely serene and unafraid she sat there with those consuming glories beating upon her.

But at last her serenity was broken up. Yes, it stood the strain of the King's gracious speech; and of D'Alençon's praiseful words, and the Bastard's; and even La Hire's thunder-blast, which took the place by storm; but at last, as I have said, they brought a force to bear which was too strong for her. For at the close the King put up his hand to command silence, and so waited, with his hand up, till every sound was dead and it was as if one could almost *feel* the stillness, so profound it was. Then out of some remote corner of that vast place there rose a plaintive voice, and in tones most tender and sweet and rich came floating through that enchanted hush our poor old simple song "L'Arbre Fée le Bourlemont!" and then Joan broke down and put her face in her hands and cried. Yes, you see, all in a moment the pomps and grandeurs dissolved away and she was a little child again herding her sheep with the tranquil pastures stretched about her, and war and wounds and blood and death and the mad frenzy and turmoil of battle a dream. Ah, that shows you the power of music, that magician of magicians, who lifts his wand and says his mysterious word and all things real pass away and the phantoms of your mind walk before you clothed in flesh.

That was the King's invention, that sweet and dear surprise. Indeed, he had fine things hidden away in his nature, though one seldom got a glimpse of them, with that scheming Tremouille and those others always standing in the light, and he so indolently content to save himself fuss and argument and let them have their way.

At the fall of night we the Domremy contingent of the personal staff were with the father and uncle at the inn, in their private parlor, brewing generous drinks and breaking ground for a homely talk about Domremy and the neighbors, when a large parcel arrived from Joan to be kept till she came; and soon she came herself and sent her guard away, saying she would take one of her father's rooms and sleep under his roof, and so be at home again. We of the staff rose and stood, as was meet, until she made us sit. Then she turned and saw that the two old men had gotten up too, and were standing in an embarrassed and unmilitary way; which made her want to laugh, but she kept it in, as not wishing to hurt them; and got them to their seats and snuggled down between them, and took a hand of each of them upon her knees and nestled her own hands in them, and said:

"Now we will have no more ceremony, but be kin and playmates as in other times; for I am done with the great wars now, and you two will take me home with you, and I shall see—" She stopped, and for a moment her happy face sobered, as if a doubt or a presentiment had flitted through her mind; then it cleared again, and she said, with a passionate yearning, "Oh, if the day were but come and we could start!"

The old father was surprised, and said:

"Why, child, are you in earnest? Would you leave doing these wonders that make you to be praised by everybody while there is still so much glory to be won; and would you go out from this grand comradeship with princes and generals to be a drudging villager again and a nobody? It is not rational."

"No," said the uncle, Laxart, "it is amazing to hear, and indeed not understandable. It is a stranger thing to hear her say she will stop the soldiering than it was to hear her say she would begin it; and I who speak to you can say in all truth that that was the strangest word that ever I had heard till this day and hour. I would it could be explained."

"It is not difficult," said Joan. "I was not ever fond of wounds and suffering, nor fitted by my nature to inflict them; and quarrelings did always distress me, and noise and tumult were against my liking, my disposition being toward peace and quietness, and love for all things that have life; and being made like this, how could I bear to think of wars and blood, and the pain that goes with them, and the sorrow and mourning that follow after? But by his angels God laid His great commands upon me, and could I disobey? I did as I was bid. Did He command me to do many things? No; only two: to raise the siege of Orleans, and crown the King at Rheims. The task is finished, and I am free. Has ever a poor soldier fallen in my sight, whether friend or foe, and I not felt his pain in my own body, and the grief of his home-mates in my own heart? No, not one; and, oh, it is such bliss to know that my release is won, and that I shall not any more see these cruel things or suffer these tortures of the mind again! Then why should I not go to my village and be as I was before? It is heaven! and ye wonder that I desire it. Ah, ye are men — just men! My mother would understand."

They didn't quite know what to say; so they sat still awhile, looking pretty vacant. Then old D'Arc said:

"Yes, your mother — that is true. I never saw

such a woman. She worries, and worries, and worries; and wakes nights, and lies so, thinking—that is, worrying; worrying about you. And when the night-storms go raging along, she moans and says, 'Ah, God pity her, she is out in this with her poor wet soldiers.' And when the lightning glares and the thunder crashes she wrings her hands and trembles, saying, 'It is like the awful cannon and the flash, and yonder somewhere she is riding down upon the spouting guns and I not there to protect her.'"

"Ah, poor mother, it is pity, it is pity!"

"Yes, a most strange woman, as I have noticed a many times. When there is news of a victory and all the village goes mad with pride and joy, she rushes here and there in a maniacal frenzy till she finds out the one only thing she cares to know—that you are safe; then down she goes on her knees in the dirt and praises God as long as there is any breath left in her body; and all on your account, for she never mentions the battle once. And always she says, '*Now* it is over—*now* France is saved—*now* she will come home'—and always is disappointed and goes about mourning."

"Don't, father! it breaks my heart. I will be so good to her when I get home. I will do her work for her, and be her comfort, and she shall not suffer any more through me."

There was some more talk of this sort, then Uncle Laxart said:

"You have done the will of God, dear, and are quits; it is true, and none may deny it; but what of the King? You are his best soldier; what if he command you to stay?"

That was a crusher — and sudden! It took Joan a moment or two to recover from the shock of it; then she said, quite simply and resignedly:

"The King is my Lord; I am his servant." She was silent and thoughtful a little while, then she brightened up and said, cheerily, "But let us drive such thoughts away — this is no time for them. Tell me about home."

So the two old gossips talked and talked; talked about everything and everybody in the village; and it was good to hear. Joan out of her kindness tried to get *us* into the conversation, but that failed, of course. She was the Commander-in-Chief, we were nobodies; her name was the mightiest in France, we were invisible atoms; she was the comrade of princes and heroes, we of the humble and obscure; she held rank above all Personages and all Puissances whatsoever in the whole earth, by right of bearing her commission direct from God. To put it in one word, she was JOAN OF ARC — and when that is said, all is said. To us she was divine. Between her and us lay the bridgeless abyss which that word implies. We could not be familiar with her. No, you can see yourselves that that would have been impossible.

And yet she was so human, too, and so good and

kind and dear and loving and cheery and charming and unspoiled and unaffected! Those are all the words I think of now, but they are not enough; no, they are too few and colorless and meager to tell it all, or tell the half. Those simple old men didn't realize her; they couldn't; they had never known any people but human beings, and so they had no other standard to measure her by. To them, after their first little shyness had worn off, she was just a girl—that was all. It was amazing. It made one shiver, sometimes, to see how calm and easy and comfortable they were in her presence, and hear them talk to her exactly as they would have talked to any other girl in France.

Why, that simple old Laxart sat up there and droned out the most tedious and empty tale one ever heard, and neither he nor Papa D'Arc ever gave a thought to the badness of the etiquette of it, or ever suspected that that foolish tale was anything but dignified and valuable history. There was not an atom of value in it; and whilst they thought it distressing and pathetic, it was in fact not pathetic at all, but actually ridiculous. At least it seemed so to me, and it seems so yet. Indeed, I know it was, because it made Joan laugh; and the more sorrowful it got the more it made her laugh; and the Paladin said that he could have laughed himself if she had not been there, and Noël Rainguesson said the same. It was about old Laxart going to a funeral there at Domremy two or three weeks back.

He had spots all over his face and hands, and he got Joan to rub some healing ointment on them, and while she was doing it, and comforting him, and trying to say pitying things to him, he told her how it happened. And first he asked her if she remembered that black bull calf that she left behind when she came away, and she said indeed she did, and he was a dear, and she loved him so, and was he well?—and just drowned him in questions about that creature. And he said it was a young bull now, and very frisky; and he was to bear a principal hand at a funeral; and she said, "The bull?" and he said, "No, myself;" but said the bull *did* take a hand, but not because of his being invited, for he wasn't; but anyway he was away over beyond the Fairy Tree, and fell asleep on the grass with his Sunday funeral clothes on, and a long black rag on his hat and hanging down his back; and when he woke he saw by the sun how late it was, and not a moment to lose; and jumped up terribly worried, and saw the young bull grazing there, and thought maybe he could ride part way on him and gain time; so he tied a rope around the bull's body to hold on by, and put a halter on him to steer with, and jumped on and started; but it was all new to the bull, and he was discontented with it, and scurried around and bellowed and reared and pranced, and Uncle Laxart was satisfied, and wanted to get off and go by the next bull or some other way that was quieter, but he didn't dare try; and it was getting very warm for him, too, and disturbing and wearisome, and not proper for Sunday; but by and by the bull lost all his temper, and went tearing down the slope with his tail in the air and bellowing in the most awful way; and just in the edge of the village he knocked down some beehives, and the bees turned out and joined the excursion, and soared along in a black cloud that nearly hid those other two from sight, and prodded them both, and jabbed them and speared them and spiked them, and made them bellow and shriek, and shriek and bellow; and here they came roaring through the village like a hurricane, and took the funeral procession right in the center, and sent that section of it sprawling, and galloped over it, and the rest scattered apart and fled screeching in every direction, every person with a layer of bees on him, and not a rag of that funeral left but the corpse; and finally the bull broke for the river and jumped in, and when they fished Uncle Laxart out he was nearly drowned, and his face looked like a pudding with raisins in it. And then he turned around, this old simpleton, and looked a long time in a dazed way at Joan where she had her face in a cushion, dying, apparently, and says:

"What do you reckon she is laughing at?"

And old D'Arc stood looking at her the same way, sort of absently scratching his head; but had to give it up, and said *he* didn't know—"must have been something that happened when we weren't noticing."

Yes, both of those old people thought that that tale was pathetic; whereas to my mind it was purely ridiculous, and not in any way valuable to any one. It seemed so to me then, and it seems so to me yet. And as for history, it does not resemble history, for the office of history is to furnish serious and important facts that *teach;* whereas this strange and useless event teaches nothing; nothing that I can see, except not to ride a bull to a funeral; and surely no reflecting person needs to be taught that.

CHAPTER XXXVII.

NOW these were nobles, you know, by decree of the King!—these precious old infants. But they did not realize it; they could not be called conscious of it; it was an abstraction, a phantom; to them it had no substance; their minds could not take hold of it. No, they did not bother about their nobility; they lived in their horses. The horses were solid; they were visible facts, and would make a mighty stir in Domremy. Presently something was said about the Coronation, and old D'Arc said it was going to be a grand thing to be able to say, when they got home, that they were present in the very town itself when it happened. Joan looked troubled, and said:

"Ah, that reminds me. You were here and you didn't send me word. In the town, indeed! Why, you could have sat with the other nobles, and been welcome; and could have looked upon the crowning itself, and carried *that* home to tell. Ah, why did you use me so, and send me no word?"

The old father was embarrassed, now, quite visibly embarrassed, and had the air of one who does not quite know what to say. But Joan was looking up in his face, her hands upon his shoulders — waiting. He had to speak; so presently he drew her to his breast, which was heaving with emotion; and he said, getting out his words with difficulty:

"There, hide your face, child, and let your old father humble himself and make his confession. I — I — don't you see, don't you understand? — I could not know that these grandeurs would not turn your young head — it would be only natural. I might shame you before these great per —"

"Father!"

"And then I was afraid, as remembering that cruel thing I said once in my sinful anger. Oh, appointed of God to be a soldier, and the greatest in the land! and in my ignorant anger I said I would drown you with my own hands if you unsexed yourself and brought shame to your name and family. Ah, how could I ever have said it, and you so good and dear and innocent! I was afraid; for I was guilty. You understand it now, my child, and you forgive?"

Do you see? Even that poor groping old land-crab, with his skull full of pulp, had pride. Isn't it wonderful? And more — he had conscience; he had a sense of right and wrong, such as it was; he was able to feel remorse. It looks impossible, it looks incredible, but it is not. I believe that some day it will be found out that peasants are people. Yes, beings in a great many respects like ourselves. And I believe that some day *they* will find this out, too — and then! Well, then I think they will rise up and demand to be regarded as part of the race, and that by consequence there will be trouble. Whenever one sees in a book or in a king's proclamation those words "the nation," they bring before us the upper classes; only those; we know no other "nation"; for us and the kings no other "nation" exists. But from the day that I saw old D'Arc the peasant acting and feeling just as I should have acted and felt myself, I have carried the conviction in my heart that our peasants are not merely animals, beasts of burden put here by the good God to produce food and comfort for the "nation," but something more and better. You look incredulous. Well, that is your training; it is the training of everybody; but as for me, I thank that incident for giving me a better light, and I have never forgotten it.

Let me see — where was I? One's mind wanders around here and there and yonder, when one is old. I think I said Joan comforted him. Certainly, that is what she would do — there was no need to say that. She coaxed him and petted him and caressed him, and laid the memory of that old hard speech of his to rest. Laid it to rest until she should be dead. Then he would remember it again — yes, yes! Lord, how those things sting, and burn, and gnaw — the things which we did against the innocent dead! And we say in our anguish, "If they could only come back!" Which is all very well to say, but, as far as I can see, it doesn't profit anything. In my opinion the best way is not to do the thing in the first place. And I am not alone in this; I have heard our two knights say the same thing; and a man there in Orleans — no, I believe it was at Beaugency, or one of those places — it seems more as if it was at Beaugency than the others — this man said the same thing exactly; almost the same words; a dark man with a cast in his eye and one leg shorter than the other. His name was — was — it is singular that I can't call that man's name; I had it in my mind only a moment ago, and I know it begins with — no, I don't remember what it begins with; but never mind, let it go; I will think of it presently, and then I will tell you.

Well, pretty soon the old father wanted to know how Joan felt when she was in the thick of a battle, with the bright blades hacking and flashing all around her, and the blows rapping and slatting on her shield, and blood gushing on her from the cloven ghastly face and broken teeth of the neighbor at her elbow, and the perilous sudden back surge of massed horses upon a person when the front ranks give way before a heavy rush of the enemy, and men tumble limp and groaning out of saddles all around, and battle-flags falling from dead hands wipe across one's face and hide the tossing turmoil a moment, and in the reeling and swaying and laboring jumble one's horse's hoofs sink into soft substances and shrieks of pain respond, and presently — panic! rush! swarm!

flight! and death and hell following after! And the old fellow got ever so much excited; and strode up and down, his tongue going like a mill, asking question after question and never waiting for an answer; and finally he stood Joan up in the middle of the room and stepped off and scanned her critcally, and said:

"No—I don't understand it. You are so little. So little and slender. When you had your armor on, to-day, it gave one a sort of notion of it; but in these pretty silks and velvets, you are only a dainty page, not a league-striding war-colossus, moving in clouds and darkness and breathing smoke and thunder. I would God I might see you at it and go tell your mother! *That* would help her sleep, poor thing! Here—teach me the arts of the soldier, that I may explain them to her."

And she did it. She gave him a pike, and put him through the manual of arms; and made him do the steps, too. His marching was incredibly awkward and slovenly, and so was his drill with the pike; but he didn't know it, and was wonderfully pleased with himself, and mightily excited and charmed with the ringing, crisp words of command. I am obliged to say that if looking proud and happy when one is marching were sufficient, he would have been the perfect soldier.

And he wanted a lesson in sword-play, and got it. But of course that was beyond him; he was too old. It was beautiful to see Joan handle the foils, but the old man was a bad failure. He was afraid of the things, and skipped and dodged and scrambled around like a woman who has lost her mind on account of the arrival of a bat. He was of no good as an exhibition. But if La Hire had only come in, that would have been another matter. Those two fenced often; I saw them many times. True, Joan was easily his master, but it made a good show for all that, for La Hire was a grand swordsman. What a swift creature Joan was! You would see her standing erect with her ankle-bones together and her foil arched over her head, the hilt in one hand and the button in the other — the old general opposite, bent forward, left hand reposing on his back, his foil advanced, slightly wiggling and squirming, his watching eye boring straight into hers — and all of a sudden she would give a spring forward, and back again; and there she was, with the foil arched over her head as before. La Hire had been hit, but all that the spectator saw of it was a something like a thin flash of light in the air, but nothing distinct, nothing definite.

We kept the drinkables moving, for that would please the Bailly and the landlord; and old Laxart and D'Arc got to feeling quite comfortable, but without being what you could call tipsy. They got out the presents which they had been buying to carry home — humble things and cheap, but they would be fine there, and welcome. And they gave to Joan a present from Père Fronte and one from her mother

— the one a little leaden image of the Holy Virgin, the other half a yard of blue silk ribbon; and she was as pleased as a child; and touched, too, as one could see plainly enough. Yes, she kissed those poor things over and over again, as if they had been something costly and wonderful; and she pinned the Virgin on her doublet, and sent for her helmet and tied the ribbon on that; first one way, then another; then a new way, then another new way; and with each effort perching the helmet on her hand and holding it off this way and that, and canting her head to one side and then the other, examining the effect, as a bird does when it has got a new bug. And she said she could almost wish she was going to the wars again; for then she would fight with the better courage, as having always with her something which her mother's touch had blessed.

Old Laxart said he hoped she would go to the wars again, but home first, for that all the people there were cruel anxious to see her — and so he went on:

"They are proud of you, dear. Yes, prouder than any village ever was of anybody before. And indeed it is right and rational; for it is the first time a village has ever had anybody like you to be proud of and call its own. And it is strange and beautiful how they try to give your name to every creature that has a sex that is convenient. It is but half a year since you began to be spoken of and left us, and so it is surprising to see how many babies there are already in that region that are named for you. First it was just Joan; then it was Joan-Orleans; then Joan-Orleans-Beaugency-Patay; and now the next ones will have a lot of towns and the Coronation added, of course. Yes, and the animals the same. They know how you love animals, and so they try to do you honor and show their love for you by naming all those creatures after you; insomuch that if a body should step out and call 'Joan of Arc — come!' there would be a landslide of cats and all such things, each supposing it was the one wanted, and all willing to take the benefit of the doubt, anyway, for the sake of the food that might be on delivery. The kitten you left behind —the last estray you fetched home — bears your name, now, and belongs to Père Fronte, and is the pet and pride of the village; and people have come miles to look at it and pet it and stare at it and wonder over it because it was Joan of Arc's cat. Everybody will tell you that; and one day when a stranger threw a stone at it, not knowing it was your cat, the village rose against him as one man and hanged him! And but for Père Fronte —"

There was an interruption. It was a messenger from the King, bearing a note for Joan, which I read to her, saying he had reflected, and had consulted his other generals, and was obliged to ask her to remain at the head of the army and withdraw her resignation. Also, would she come immediately and attend a council of war? Straightway, at a little distance, military commands and the rumble of drums broke on the still night, and we knew that her guard was approaching.

Deep disappointment clouded her face for just one moment and no more—it passed, and with it the homesick girl, and she was Joan of Arc, Commander-in-Chief again, and ready for duty.

CHAPTER XXXVIII.

IN my double quality of page and secretary I followed Joan to the council. She entered that presence with the bearing of a grieved goddess. What was become of the volatile child that so lately was enchanted with a ribbon and suffocated with laughter over the distresses of a foolish peasant who had stormed a funeral on the back of a bee-stung bull? One may not guess. Simply it was gone, and had left no sign. She moved straight to the council-table, and stood. Her glance swept from face to face there, and where it fell, these it lit as with a torch, those it scorched as with a brand. She knew where to strike. She indicated the generals with a nod, and said:

"My business is not with you. You have not craved a council of war." Then she turned toward the King's privy council, and continued: "No; it is with you. A council of war! It is amazing. There is but one thing to do, and only one, and lo, ye call a council of war! Councils of war have no value but to decide between two or several doubtful courses. But a council of war when there is only *one* course? Conceive of a man in a boat and his family in the water, and he goes out among his friends to ask what he would better do? A council of war, name of God! To determine what?"

She stopped, and turned till her eyes rested upon the face of La Tremouille; and so she stood, silent, measuring him, the excitement in all faces burning steadily higher and higher, and all pulses beating faster and faster; then she said, with deliberation:

"Every sane man—whose loyalty to his King is not a show and a pretence—knows that there is but one rational thing before us—*the march upon Paris!*"

Down came the fist of La Hire with an approving crash upon the table. La Tremouille turned white with anger, but he pulled himself firmly together and held his peace. The King's lazy blood was stirred and his eye kindled finely, for the spirit of war was away down in him somewhere, and a frank, bold speech always found it and made it tingle gladsomely. Joan waited to see if the chief minister might wish to defend his position; but he was experienced and wise, and not a man to waste his forces where the current was against him. He would wait; the King's private ear would be at his disposal by and by.

That pious fox the Chancellor of France took the word now. He washed his soft hands together, smiling persuasively, and said to Joan:

"Would it be courteous, your Excellency, to

move abruptly from here without waiting for an answer from the Duke of Burgundy? You may not know that we are negotiating with his Highness, and that there is likely to be a fortnight's truce between us; and on his part a pledge to deliver Paris into our hands without cost of a blow or the fatigue of a march thither."

Joan turned to him and said, gravely:

"This is not a confessional, my lord. You were not obliged to expose that shame here."

The Chancellor's face reddened, and he retorted:

"Shame? What is there shameful about it?"

Joan answered in level, passionless tones:

"One may describe it without hunting far for words. I knew of this poor comedy, my lord, although it was not intended that I should know. It is to the credit of the devisers of it that they tried to conceal it—this comedy whose text and impulse are describable in two words."

The Chancellor spoke up with a fine irony in his manner:

"Indeed? And will your Excellency be good enough to utter them?"

"Cowardice and treachery!"

The fists of all the generals came down this time, and again the King's eye sparkled with pleasure. The Chancellor sprang to his feet and appealed to his Majesty:

"Sire, I claim your protection."

But the King waved him to his seat again, saying:

"Peace. She had a right to be consulted before that thing was undertaken, since it concerned war as well as politics. It is but just that she be heard upon it now."

The Chancellor sat down trembling with indignation, and remarked to Joan:

"Out of charity I will consider that you did not know who devised this measure which you condemn in so candid language."

"Save your charity for another occasion, my lord," said Joan, as calmly as before. "Whenever anything is done to injure the interests and degrade the honor of France, all but the dead know how to name the two conspirators-in-chief—"

"Sire, sire! this insinuation—"

"It is not an insinuation, my lord," said Joan, placidly, "it is a charge. I bring it against the King's chief minister and his Chancellor."

Both men were on their feet now, insisting that the King modify Joan's frankness; but he was not minded to do it. His ordinary councils were stale water—his spirit was drinking wine, now, and the taste of it was good. He said:

"Sit—and be patient. What is fair for one must in fairness be allowed the other. Consider—and be just. When have you two spared her? What dark charges and harsh names have you withheld when you spoke of her?" Then he added, with a veiled twinkle in his eye, "If these are offenses I see no particular difference between them, except that she says her hard things to your faces, whereas you say yours behind her back."

He was pleased with that neat shot and the way it shriveled those two people up, and made La Hire laugh out loud and the other generals softly quake and chuckle. Joan tranquilly resumed:

"From the first, we have been hindered by this policy of shilly-shally; this fashion of counseling and counseling and counseling where no counseling is needed, but only fighting. We took Orleans on the 8th of May, and could have cleared the region round about in three days and saved the slaughter of Patay. We could have been in Rheims six weeks ago, and in Paris now; and would see the last Englishman pass out of France in half a year. But we struck no blow after Orleans, but went off into the country—what for? Ostensibly to hold councils; really to give Bedford time to send reinforcements to Talbot—which he did; and Patay had to be fought. After Patay, more counseling, more waste of precious time. Oh, my King, I would that you would be persuaded!" She began to warm up, now. "Once more we have our opportunity. If we rise and strike, all is well. Bid me march upon Paris. In twenty days it shall be yours, and in six months all France! Here is half a year's work before us; if this chance be wasted, I give you twenty years to do it in. Speak the word, O gentle King—speak but the one—"

"I cry you mercy!" interrupted the Chancellor,

who saw a dangerous enthusiasm rising in the King's face. "March upon Paris? Does your Excellency forget that the way bristles with English strongholds?"

"*That* for your English strongholds!" and Joan snapped her fingers scornfully. "Whence have we marched in these last days? From Gien. And whither? To Rheims. What bristled between? English strongholds. What are they now? French ones—and they never cost a blow!" Here applause broke out from the group of generals, and Joan had to pause a moment to let it subside. "Yes, English strongholds bristled before us; now French ones bristle behind us. What is the argument? A child can read it. The strongholds between us and Paris are garrisoned by no new breed of English, but by the same breed as those others—with the same fears, the same questionings, the same weaknesses, the same disposition to see the heavy hand of God descending upon them. We have but to march!—on the instant—and they are ours, Paris is ours, France is ours! Give the word, O my King, command your servant to—"

"Stay!" cried the Chancellor. "It would be madness to put this affront upon his Highness the Duke of Burgundy. By the treaty which we have every hope to make with him—"

"Oh, the treaty which we hope to make with him! He has scorned you for years, and defied you. Is it your subtle persuasions that have softened his manners and beguiled him to listen to proposals? No; it was *blows!*—the blows which *we* gave him! That is the only teaching that that sturdy rebel can understand. What does he care for *wind?* The treaty which we hope to make with him—alack! *He* deliver Paris! There is no pauper in the land that is less able to do it. He deliver Paris! Ah, but that would make great Bedford smile! Oh, the pitiful pretext! the blind can see that this thin pourparler with its fifteen-day truce has no purpose but to give Bedford time to hurry forward his forces against us. More treachery—always treachery! We call a council of war—with nothing to council about; but Bedford calls no council to teach him what our one course is. He knows what he would do in our place. *He would hang his traitors and march upon Paris!* O gentle King, rouse! The way is open, Paris beckons, France implores. Speak and we—"

"Sire, it is madness, sheer madness! Your Excellency, we cannot, we must not go back from what we have done; we have proposed to treat, we *must* treat with the Duke of Burgundy."

"And we *will?* said Joan.

"Ah? How?"

"*At the point of the lance!*"

The house rose, to a man—all that had French hearts—and let go a crash of applause—and kept it up; and in the midst of it one heard La Hire growl out: "At the point of the lance! By God, that is the music!" The King was up, too, and drew his sword, and took it by the blade and strode to Joan and delivered the hilt of it into her hand, saying:

"There, the King surrenders. Carry it to Paris."

And so the applause burst out again, and the historical council of war that has bred so many legends was over.

CHAPTER XXXIX.

IT was away past midnight, and had been a tremendous day in the matter of excitement and fatigue, but that was no matter to Joan when there was business on hand. She did not think of bed. The generals followed her to her official quarters, and she delivered her orders to them as fast as she could talk, and they sent them off to their different commands as fast as delivered; wherefore the messengers galloping hither and thither raised a world of clatter and racket in the still streets; and soon were added to this the music of distant bugles and the roll of drums — notes of preparation; for the vanguard would break camp at dawn.

The generals were soon dismissed, but I wasn't; nor Joan; for it was my turn to work, now. Joan walked the floor and dictated a summons to the Duke of Burgundy to lay down his arms and make peace and exchange pardons with the King; or, if he *must* fight, go fight the Saracens. "Pardonnez-vous l'un à l'autre de bon cœur, entièrement, ainsi que doivent faire loyaux chrétiens, et, s'il vous plait de guerroyer, allez contre les Sarrasins." It was long, but it was good, and had the sterling ring to it. It is my opinion that it was as fine and simple and straightforward and eloquent a state paper as she ever uttered.

It was delivered into the hands of a courier, and he galloped away with it. Then Joan dismissed me, and told me to go to the inn and stay, and in the morning give to her father the parcel which she had left there. It contained presents for the Domremy relatives and friends and a peasant dress which she had bought for herself. She said she would say good-bye to her father and uncle in the morning if it should still be their purpose to go, instead of tarrying awhile to see the city.

I didn't say anything, of course: but I could have said that wild horses couldn't keep those men in that town half a day. *They* waste the glory of being the first to carry the great news to Domremy — *the taxes remitted forever!* — and hear the bells clang and clatter, and the people cheer and shout? Oh, not they. Patay and Orleans and the Coronation were events which in a vague way these men understood to be colossal; but they were colossal mists, films, abstractions: *this* was a gigantic reality!

When I got there, do you suppose they were abed! Quite the reverse. They and the rest were as mellow as mellow could be; and the Paladin was doing his battles over in great style, and the old peasants were endangering the building with their applause. He was doing Patay now; and was bending his big frame forward and laying out the positions and movements with a rake here and a rake there of his formidable sword on the floor, and the peasants were stooped over with their hands on their spread knees observing with excited eyes and ripping out ejaculations of wonder and admiration all along:

"Yes, here we were, waiting—waiting for the word; our horses fidgeting and snorting and dancing to get away, we lying back on the bridles till our bodies fairly slanted to the rear; the word rang out at last—'*Go!*' and we went!

"Went? There was nothing like it ever seen! Where we swept by squads of scampering English, the mere wind of our passage laid them flat in piles and rows! Then we plunged into the ruck of Fastolfe's frantic battle-corps and tore through it like a hurricane, leaving a causeway of the dead stretching far behind; no tarrying, no slacking rein, but on! on! on! far yonder in the distance lay *our* prey—Talbot and his host looming vast and dark like a storm-cloud brooding on the sea! Down we swooped upon them, glooming all the air with a quivering pall of dead leaves flung up by the whirlwind of our flight. In another moment we should have struck them as world strikes world when disorbited constellations crash into the Milky Way, but by misfortune and the inscrutable dispensation of God I was recognized! Talbot turned white, and shouting, 'Save yourselves, it is the Standard-Bearer of Joan of Arc!' drove his spurs home till they met in the middle of his horse's entrails, and fled the field with his billowing multitudes at his back! I could have cursed myself for not putting on a disguise.' I saw reproach in the eyes of her Excellency, and was bitterly ashamed. I had caused what seemed an irreparable disaster. Another might have gone aside to grieve, as not seeing any way to mend it; but I thank God I am not of those. Great occasions only summon as with a trumpet-call the slumbering reserves of my intellect. I saw my opportunity in an instant—in the next I was away! Through the woods I vanished—*fst!*—like an extinguished light! Away around through the curtaining forest I sped, as if on wings, none knowing what was become of me, none suspecting my design. Minute after minute passed, on and on I flew; on, and still on; and at last with a great cheer I flung my Banner to the breeze and burst out in *front* of Talbot! Oh, it was a mighty thought! That weltering chaos of distracted men whirled and surged backward like a tidal wave which has struck a continent, and the day was ours! Poor helpless creatures, they were in a trap; they were surrounded; they could not escape to the rear, for there was our army; they could not escape to the front, for there was I. Their hearts shriveled in their bodies, their hands fell listless at their sides. They stood still, and at our leisure we slaughtered them to a man; all except Talbot and Fastolfe, whom I saved and brought away, one under each arm."

Well, there is no denying it, the Paladin was in great form that night. Such style! such noble grace of gesture, such grandeur of attitude, such energy when he got going! such steady rise, on such sure wing, such nicely graduated expenditures of voice according to weight of matter, such skillfully calculated approaches to his surprises and explosions, such belief-compelling sincerity of tone and manner, such a climaxing peal from his brazen lungs, and such a lightning-vivid picture of his mailed form and flaunting banner when he burst out before that despairing army! And oh, the gentle art of the last half of his last sentence—delivered in the careless and indolent tone of one who has finished his real story, and only adds a colorless and inconsequential detail because it has happened to occur to him in a lazy way.

It was a marvel to see those innocent peasants. Why, they went all to pieces with enthusiasm, and roared out applauses fit to raise the roof and wake the dead. When they had cooled down at last and there was silence but for the heaving and panting, old Laxart said, admiringly:

"As it seems to me, you are an army in your single person."

"Yes, that is what he is," said Noël Rainguesson, convincingly. "He is a terror; and not just in *this* vicinity. His mere name carries a shudder with it to distant lands—just his mere name; and when he frowns, the shadow of it falls as far as Rome, and the chickens go to roost an hour before schedule time. Yes; and some say—"

"Noël Rainguesson, you are preparing yourself for trouble. I will say just one word to you, and it will be to your advantage to—"

I saw that the usual thing had got a start. No man could prophesy when it would end. So I delivered Joan's message and went off to bed.

Joan made her good-byes to those old fellows in the morning, with loving embraces and many tears, and with a packed multitude for sympathizers, and they rode proudly away on their precious horses to carry their great news home. I had seen better riders, I will say that; for horsemanship was a new art to them.

The vanguard moved out at dawn and took the road, with bands braying and banners flying; the second division followed at eight. Then came the Burgundian ambassadors, and lost us the rest of that day and the whole of the next. But Joan was on hand, and so they had their journey for their pains. The rest of us took the road at dawn, next morning, July 20th. And got how far? Six leagues. Tremouille was getting in his sly work with the vacillating King, you see. The King stopped at St. Marcoul and prayed three days. Precious time lost—for us; precious time gained for Bedford. He would know how to use it.

We could not go on without the King; that would be to leave him in the conspirators' camp. Joan argued, reasoned, implored; and at last we got under way again.

Joan's prediction was verified. It was not a campaign, it was only another holiday excursion. English strongholds lined our route; they surrendered without a blow; we garrisoned them with Frenchmen and passed on. Bedford was on the march against us with his new army by this time, and on the 25th of July the hostile forces faced each other and made preparation for battle; but Bedford's good judgment prevailed, and he turned and retreated toward Paris. Now was our chance. Our men were in great spirits.

Will you believe it? Our poor stick of a King allowed his worthless advisers to persuade him to start back for Gien, whence he had set out when we first marched for Rheims and the Coronation! And we actually did start back. The fifteen-day truce had just been concluded with the Duke of Burgundy, and we would go and tarry at Gien until he should deliver Paris to us without a fight.

We marched to Bray; then the King changed his mind once more, and with it his face toward Paris. Joan dictated a letter to the citizens of Rheims to encourage them to keep heart in spite of the truce, and promising to stand by them. She furnished them the news herself that the King had made this truce; and in speaking of it she was her usual frank self. She said she was not satisfied with it, and didn't know whether she would keep it or not; that if she kept it, it would be solely out of tenderness for the King's honor. All French children know those famous words. How naïve they are! "De cette trève qui a été faite, je ne suis pas contente, et je ne sais si je la tiendrai. Si je la tiens, ce sera seulement pour garder l'honneur du roi." But in any case, she said, she would not allow the blood royal to be abused, and would keep the army in good order and ready for work at the end of the truce.

Poor child, to have to fight England, Burgundy, and a French conspiracy all at the same time—it was too bad. She was a match for the others, but a conspiracy—ah, nobody is a match for that, when the victim that is to be injured is weak and willing. It grieved her, these troubled days, to be so hindered and delayed and baffled, and at times she was sad and the tears lay near the surface. Once, talking with her good old faithful friend and servant, the Bastard of Orleans, she said:

"Ah, if it might but please God to let me put off this steel raiment and go back to my father and my mother, and tend my sheep again with my sister and my brothers, who would be so glad to see me!"

By the 12th of August we were camped near Dampmartin. Later we had a brush with Bedford's rear-guard, and had hopes of a big battle on the morrow, but Bedford and all his force got away in the night and went on toward Paris.

Charles sent heralds and received the submission

of Beauvais. The Bishop Pierre Cauchon, that faithful friend and slave of the English, was not able to prevent it, though he did his best. He was obscure then, but his name was to travel round the globe presently, and live forever in the curses of France! Bear with me now, while I spit in fancy upon his grave.

Compiègne surrendered, and hauled down the English flag. On the 14th we camped two leagues from Senlis. Bedford turned and approached, and took up a strong position. We went against him, but all our efforts to beguile him out from his entrenchments failed, though he had promised us a duel in the open field. Night shut down. Let him look out for the morning! But in the morning he was gone again.

We entered Compiègne the 18th of August, turning out the English garrison and hoisting our own flag.

On the 23d Joan gave command to move upon Paris. The King and the clique were not satisfied with this, and retired sulking to Senlis, which had just surrendered. Within a few days many strong places submitted — Creil, Pont-Saint-Maxence, Choisy, Gournay-sur-Aronde, Remy, La Neufville-en-Hez, Moguay, Chantilly, Saintines. The English power was tumbling, crash after crash! And still the King sulked and disapproved, and was afraid of our movement against the capital.

On the 26th of August, 1429, Joan camped at Saint Denis; in effect, under the walls of Paris.

And still the King hung back and was afraid. If we could but have had him there to back us with his authority! Bedford had lost heart and decided to waive resistance and go and concentrate his strength in the best and loyalest province remaining to him — Normandy. Ah, if we could only have persuaded the King to come and countenance us with his presence and approval at this supreme moment!

CHAPTER XL.

COURIER after courier was despatched to the King, and he promised to come, but didn't. The Duke d'Alençon went to him and got his promise again, which he broke again. Nine days were lost thus; then he came, arriving at St. Denis September 7th.

Meantime the enemy had begun to take heart: the spiritless conduct of the King could have no other result. Preparations had now been made to defend the city. Joan's chances had been diminished, but she and her generals considered them plenty good enough yet. Joan ordered the attack for eight o'clock next morning, and at that hour it began.

Joan placed her artillery and began to pound a strong work which protected the gate St. Honoré. When it was sufficiently crippled the assault was sounded at noon, and it was carried by storm. Then we moved forward to storm the gate itself, and hurled ourselves against it again and again, Joan in the lead with her standard at her side, the smoke enveloping us in choking clouds, and the missiles flying over us and through us as thick as hail.

In the midst of our last assault, which would have

carried the gate sure and given us Paris and in effect France, Joan was struck down by a crossbow bolt, and our men fell back instantly and almost in a panic —for what were they without her? *She* was the army, herself.

Although disabled, she refused to retire, and begged that a new assault be made, saying it *must* win; and adding, with the battle-light rising in her eyes, "I will take Paris now or die!" She had to be carried away by force, and this was done by Gaucourt and the Duke d'Alençon.

But her spirits were at the very top notch, now. She was brimming with enthusiasm. She said she would be carried before the gate in the morning, and in half an hour Paris would be ours without any question. She could have kept her word. About this there was no doubt. But she forgot one factor— the King, shadow of that substance named La Tremouille. The King forbade the attempt!

You see, a new Embassy had just come from the Duke of Burgundy, and another sham private trade of some sort was on foot.

You would know, without my telling you, that Joan's heart was nearly broken. Because of the pain of her wound and the pain at her heart she slept little that night. Several times the watchers heard muffled sobs from the dark room where she lay at St. Denis, and many times the grieving words "It could have been taken!—it could have been taken!" which were the only ones she said.

She dragged herself out of bed a day later with a new hope. D'Alençon had thrown a bridge across the Seine near St. Denis. Might she not cross by that and assault Paris at another point? But the King got wind of it and broke the bridge down! And more — he declared the campaign ended! And more still — he had made a new truce and a long one, in which he had agreed to leave Paris unthreatened and unmolested, and go back to the Loire whence he had come!

Joan of Arc, who had never been defeated by the enemy, was defeated by her own King. She had said once that all she feared for her cause was treachery. It had struck its first blow now. She hung up her white armor in the royal basilica of St. Denis, and went and asked the King to relieve her of her functions and let her go home. As usual, she was wise. Grand combinations, far-reaching great military moves were at an end, now; for the future, when the truce should end, the war would be merely a war of random and idle skirmishes, apparently; work suitable for subalterns, and not requiring the supervision of a sublime military genius. But the King would not let her go. The truce did not embrace all France; there were French strongholds to be watched and preserved; he would need her. Really you see, Tremouille wanted to keep her where he could balk and hinder her.

Now came her Voices again. They said, "*Remain at St. Denis.*" There was no explanation.

They did not say why. That was the voice of God; it took precedence of the command of the King; Joan resolved to stay. But that filled La Tremouille with dread. She was too tremendous a force to be left to herself; she would surely defeat all his plans. He beguiled the King to use compulsion. Joan had to submit — because she was wounded and helpless. In the Great Trial she said she was carried away against her will; and that if she had not been wounded it could not have been accomplished. Ah, she had a spirit, that slender girl! a spirit to brave all earthly powers and defy them. We shall never know why the Voices ordered her to stay. We only know this: that if she could have obeyed, the history of France would not be as it now stands written in the books. Yes, well we know that.

On the 13th of September the army, sad and spiritless, turned its face toward the Loire, and marched — without music! Yes, one noted that detail. It was a funeral march; that is what it was. A long, dreary funeral march, with never a shout or a cheer; friends looking on in tears, all the way, enemies laughing. We reached Gien at last — that place whence we had set out on our splendid march toward Rheims less than three months before, with flags flying, bands playing, the victory-flush of Patay glowing in our faces, and the massed multitudes shouting and praising and giving us God-speed. There was a dull rain falling now, the day was dark, the heavens mourned, the spectators were few, we had no welcome but the welcome of silence, and pity, and tears.

Then the King disbanded that noble army of heroes; it furled its flags, it stored its arms: the disgrace of France was complete. La Tremouille wore the victor's crown; Joan of Arc, the unconquerable, was conquered.

CHAPTER XLI.

YES, it was as I have said: Joan had Paris and France in her grip, and the Hundred Years' War under her heel, and the King made her open her fist and take away her foot.

Now followed about eight months of drifting about with the King and his council, and his gay and showy and dancing and flirting and hawking and frolicking and serenading and dissipating court—drifting from town to town and from castle to castle—a life which was pleasant to us of the personal staff, but not to Joan. However, she only *saw* it, she didn't live it. The King did his sincerest best to make her happy, and showed a most kind and constant anxiety in this matter. All others had to go loaded with the chains of an exacting court etiquette, but she was free, she was privileged. So that she paid her duty to the King once a day and passed the pleasant word, nothing further was required of her. Naturally, then, she made herself a hermit, and grieved the weary days through in her own apartments, with her thoughts and devotions for company, and the planning of now forever unrealizable military combinations for entertainment. In fancy she moved bodies of men from this and that and the other point, so calculating the distances to be covered, the time required for each body, and the nature of the country to be traversed, as to have them appear in sight of each other on a given day or at a given hour and concentrate for battle. It was her only game, her only relief from her burden of sorrow and inaction. She played it hour after hour, as others play chess; and lost herself in it, and so got repose for her mind and healing for her heart.

She never complained, of course. It was not her way. She was the sort that endure in silence. But—she was a caged eagle just the same, and pined for the free air and the alpine heights and the fierce joys of the storm.

France was full of rovers—disbanded soldiers ready for anything that might turn up. Several times, at intervals, when Joan's dull captivity grew too heavy to bear, she was allowed to gather a troop of cavalry and make a health-restoring dash against the enemy. These things were like a bath to her spirits.

It was like old times, there at Saint-Pierre-le-Moutier, to see her lead assault after assault, be driven back again and again, but always rally and charge anew, all in a blaze of eagerness and delight; till at last the tempest of missiles rained so intolerably thick that old D'Aulon, who was wounded, sounded the retreat (for the King had charged him on his head to let no harm come to Joan); and away everybody rushed after him — as he supposed; but when he turned and looked, there were we of the staff still hammering away; wherefore he rode back and urged her to come, saying she was mad to stay there with only a dozen men. Her eye danced merrily, and she turned upon him crying out:

"A dozen men! name of God, I have fifty thousand, and will never budge till this place is taken! Sound the charge!"

Which he did, and over the walls we went, and the fortress was ours. Old D'Aulon thought her mind was wandering; but all she meant was, that she felt the might of fifty thousand men surging in her heart. It was a fanciful expression; but, to my thinking, truer word was never said.

Then there was the affair near Lagny, where we charged the intrenched Burgundians through the open field four times, the last time victoriously; the best prize of it Franquet d'Arras, the freebooter and pitiless scourge of the region roundabout.

Now and then other such affairs; and at last, away toward the end of May, 1430, we were in the neighborhood of Compiègne, and Joan resolved to go to the help of that place, which was being besieged by the Duke of Burgundy.

I had been wounded lately, and was not able to ride without help; but the good Dwarf took me on behind him, and I held on to him and was safe enough. We started at midnight, in a sullen downpour of warm rain, and went slowly and softly and in dead silence, for we had to slip through the enemy's lines. We were challenged only once; we made no answer, but held our breath and crept steadily and stealthily along, and got through without any accident. About three or half past we reached Compiègne, just as the gray dawn was breaking in the East.

Joan set to work at once, and concerted a plan with Guillaume de Flavy, captain of the city — a plan for a sortie toward evening against the enemy, who was posted in three bodies on the other side of the Oise, in the level plain. From our side one of the city gates communicated with a bridge. The end of this bridge was defended on the other side of the river by one of those fortresses called a boulevard; and this boulevard also commanded a raised road, which stretched from its front across the plain to the village of Marguy. A force of Burgundians occupied Marguy; another was camped at Clairoix, a couple of miles *above* the raised road; and a body of English was holding Venette, a mile and a half *below* it. A kind of bow-and-arrow arrangement, you see: the causeway the arrow, the boulevard at the feather-end of it, Marguy at the barb, Venette at one end of the bow, Clairoix at the other.

Joan's plan was to go straight per causeway against Marguy, carry it by assault, then turn swiftly upon Clairoix, up to the right, and capture that camp in the same way, then face to the rear and be ready for heavy work, for the Duke of Burgundy lay behind Clairoix with a reserve. Flavy's lieutenant, with archers and the artillery of the boulevard, was to keep the English troops from coming up from below and seizing the causeway and cutting off Joan's retreat in case she should have to make one. Also, a fleet of covered boats was to be stationed near the boulevard as an additional help in case a retreat should become necessary.

It was the 24th of May. At four in the afternoon Joan moved out at the head of six hundred cavalry — on her last march in this life!

It breaks my heart. I had got myself helped up on to the walls, and from there I saw much that happened, the rest was told me long afterward by our two knights and other eye-witnesses. Joan crossed the bridge, and soon left the boulevard behind her and went skimming away over the raised road with her horsemen clattering at her heels. She had on a brilliant silver-gilt cape over her armor, and I could see it flap and flare and rise and fall like a little patch of white flame.

It was a bright day, and one could see far and wide over that plain. Soon we saw the English force advancing, swiftly and in handsome order, the sunlight flashing from its arms.

Joan crashed into the Burgundians at Marguy and was repulsed. Then she saw the other Burgundians moving down from Clairoix. Joan rallied her men and charged again, and was again rolled back. Two assaults occupy a good deal of time — and time was precious here. The English were approaching the road now from Venette, but the boulevard opened fire on them and they were checked. Joan heartened her men with inspiring words and led them to the charge again in great style. This time she carried Marguy with a hurrah. Then she turned at once to the right and plunged into the plain and struck the Clairoix force, which was just arriving; then there was heavy work, and plenty of it, the two armies hurling each other backward turn about and about, and victory inclining first to the one, then to the other. Now all of a sudden there was a panic on our side. Some say one thing caused it, some another. Some say the cannonade made our front ranks think retreat was being cut off by the English, some say the rear ranks got the idea that Joan was killed. Anyway our men broke, and went flying in a wild rout for the causeway. Joan tried to rally them and face them around, crying to them that victory was sure, but it did no good, they divided and swept by her like a wave. Old D'Aulon begged her to retreat while there was yet a chance for safety, but she refused; so he seized her horse's bridle and bore her along with the wreck and ruin in spite of herself. And so along the causeway they came swarming, that wild confusion of frenzied men and horses — and the artillery had to stop firing, of course; consequently the English and Burgundians closed in in safety, the former in front, the latter behind their prey. Clear to the boulevard the French were washed in this enveloping inundation; and there, cornered in an angle formed by the flank of the boulevard and the slope of the causeway, they bravely fought a hopeless fight, and sank down one by one.

Flavy, watching from the city wall, ordered the gate to be closed and the drawbridge raised. This shut Joan out.

The little personal guard around her thinned swiftly. Both of our good knights went down disabled; Joan's two brothers fell wounded; then Noël Rainguesson — all wounded while loyally sheltering Joan from blows aimed at her. When only the Dwarf and the Paladin were left, they would not give up, but stood their ground stoutly, a pair of steel towers streaked and splashed with blood; and where the axe of the one fell, and the sword of the other, an enemy gasped and died. And so fighting, and loyal to their duty to the last, good simple souls, they came to their honorable end. Peace to their memories! they were very dear to me.

Then there was a cheer and a rush, and Joan, still defiant, still laying about her with her sword, was seized by her cape and dragged from her horse. She was borne away a prisoner to the Duke of Burgundy's camp, and after her followed the victorious army roaring its joy.

The awful news started instantly on its round;

from lip to lip it flew; and wherever it came it struck the people as with a sort of paralysis; and they murmured over and over again, as if they were talking to themselves, or in their sleep, "The Maid of Orleans taken!......Joan of Arc a prisoner! ......the Saviour of France lost to us!"—and would keep saying that over, as if they couldn't understand how it could be, or how God could permit it, poor creatures!

You know what a city is like when it is hung from eaves to pavement with rustling black? Then you know what Tours was like, and some other cities. But can any man tell you what the mourning in the hearts of the peasantry of France was like? No, nobody can tell you that, and, poor dumb things, they could not have told you themselves, but it was there—indeed, yes. Why, it was the spirit of a whole nation hung with crape!

The 24th of May. We will draw down the curtain now upon the most strange, and pathetic, and wonderful military drama that has been played upon the stage of the world. Joan of Arc will march no more.

Book III

TRIAL AND MARTYRDOM

CHAPTER I.

I CANNOT bear to dwell at great length upon the shameful history of the summer and winter following the capture. For a while I was not much troubled, for I was expecting every day to hear that Joan had been put to ransom, and that the King — no, not the King, but grateful France — had come eagerly forward to pay it. By the laws of war she could not be denied the privilege of ransom. She was not a rebel; she was a legitimately constituted soldier, head of the armies of France by her King's appointment, and guilty of no crime known to military law; therefore she could not be detained upon any pretext, if ransom were proffered.

But day after day dragged by and no ransom was offered! It seems incredible, but it is true. Was that reptile Tremouille busy at the King's ear? All we know is, that the King was silent, and made no offer and no effort in behalf of this poor girl who had done so much for him.

But, unhappily, there was alacrity enough in another quarter. The news of the capture reached Paris the day after it happened, and the glad English and Burgundians deafened the world all the day and all the night with the clamor of their joy-bells and the thankful thunder of their artillery, and the next day the Vicar-General of the Inquisition sent a message to the Duke of Burgundy requiring the delivery of the prisoner into the hands of the Church to be tried as an idolater.

The English had seen their opportunity, and it was the English power that was really acting, not the Church. The Church was being used as a blind, a disguise; and for a forcible reason: the Church was not only able to take the life of Joan of Arc, but to blight her influence and the valor-breeding inspiration of her name, whereas the English power could but kill her body; that would not diminish or destroy the influence of her name; it would magnify it and make it permanent. Joan of Arc was the only power in France that the English did not despise, the only power in France that they considered formidable. If the Church could be brought to take her life, or to proclaim her an idolater, a heretic, a witch, sent from Satan, not from heaven, it was believed that the English supremacy could be at once reinstated.

The Duke of Burgundy listened—but waited. He could not doubt that the French King or the French people would come forward presently and pay a higher price than the English. He kept Joan a close prisoner in a strong fortress, and continued to wait, week after week. He was a French prince, and was at heart ashamed to sell her to the English. Yet with all his waiting no offer came to him from the French side.

One day Joan played a cunning trick on her jailer, and not only slipped out of her prison, but locked him up in it. But as she fled away she was seen by a sentinel, and was caught and brought back.

Then she was sent to Beaurevoir, a stronger castle. This was early in August, and she had been in captivity more than two months now. Here she was shut up in the top of a tower which was sixty feet high. She ate her heart there for another long stretch — about three months and a half. And she was aware, all these weary five months of captivity, that the English, under cover of the Church, were dickering for her as one would dicker for a horse or a slave, and that France was silent, the King silent, all her friends the same. Yes, it was pitiful.

And yet when she heard at last that Compiègne was being closely besieged and likely to be captured, and that the enemy had declared that no inhabitant of it should escape massacre, not even children of seven years of age, she was in a fever at once to fly to our rescue. So she tore her bed clothes to strips and tied them together and descended this frail rope in the night, and it broke, and she fell and was badly bruised, and remained three days insensible, meantime neither eating nor drinking.

And now came relief to us, led by the Count of

Vendôme, and Compiègne was saved and the siege raised. This was a disaster to the Duke of Burgundy. He had to have money now. It was a good time for a new bid to be made for Joan of Arc. The English at once sent a French Bishop — that forever infamous Pierre Cauchon of Beauvais. He was partly promised the Archbishopric of Rouen, which was vacant, if he should succeed. He claimed the right to preside over Joan's ecclesiastical trial because the battle-ground where she was taken was within his diocese.

By the military usage of the time the ransom of a royal prince was 10,000 livres of gold, which is 61,125 francs — a fixed sum, you see. It must be accepted when offered; it could not be refused.

Cauchon brought the offer of this very sum from the English — a royal prince's ransom for the poor little peasant girl of Domremy. It shows in a striking way the English idea of her formidable importance. It was accepted. For that sum Joan of Arc, the Saviour of France, was sold; sold to her enemies; to the enemies of her country; enemies who had lashed and thrashed and thumped and trounced France for a century and made holiday sport of it; enemies who had forgotten, years and years ago, what a Frenchman's face was like, so used were they to seeing nothing but his back; enemies whom she had whipped, whom she had cowed, whom she had taught to respect French valor, new-born in her nation by the breath of her spirit; enemies who hungered for her life as being the only puissance able to stand between English triumph and French degradation. Sold to a French priest by a French prince, with the French King and the French nation standing thankless by and saying nothing.

And she — what did she say? Nothing. Not a reproach passed her lips. She was too great for that — she was Joan of Arc; and when that is said, all is said.

As a soldier, her record was spotless. She could not be called to account for anything under that head. A subterfuge must be found, and, as we have seen, was found. She must be tried by priests for crimes against religion. If none could be discovered, some must be invented. Let the miscreant Cauchon alone to contrive those.

Rouen was chosen as the scene of the trial. It was in the heart of the English power; its population had been under English dominion so many generations that they were hardly French now, save in language. The place was strongly garrisoned. Joan was taken there near the end of December, 1430, and flung into a dungeon. Yes, and clothed in chains, that free spirit!

Still France made no move. How do I account for this? I think there is only one way. You will remember that whenever Joan was not at the front, the French held back and ventured nothing; that whenever she led, they swept everything before them, so long as they could see her white armor or her banner; that every time she fell wounded or was reported killed — as at Compiègne — they broke in panic and fled like sheep. I argue from this that they had undergone no real transformation as yet; that at bottom they were still under the spell of a timorousness born of generations of unsuccess, and a lack of confidence in each other and in their leaders born of old and bitter experience in the way of treacheries of all sorts — for their kings had been treacherous to their great vassals and to their generals, and these in turn were treacherous to the head of the state and to each other. The soldiery found that they could depend utterly on Joan, and upon her alone. With her gone, everything was gone. She was the sun that melted the frozen torrents and set them boiling; with that sun removed, they froze again, and the army and all France became what they had been before, mere dead corpses — that and nothing more; incapable of thought, hope, ambition, or motion.

CHAPTER II.

MY wound gave me a great deal of trouble clear into the first part of October; then the fresher weather renewed my life and strength. All this time there were reports drifting about that the King was going to ransom Joan. I believed these, for I was young and had not yet found out the littleness and meanness of our poor human race, which brags about itself so much, and thinks it is better and higher than the other animals.

In October I was well enough to go out with two sorties, and in the second one, on the 23d, I was wounded again. My luck had turned, you see. On the night of the 25th the besiegers decamped, and in the disorder and confusion one of their prisoners escaped and got safe into Compiègne, and hobbled into my room as pallid and pathetic an object as you would wish to see.

"What? Alive? Noël Rainguesson!"

It was indeed he. It was a most joyful meeting, that you will easily know; and also as sad as it was joyful. We could not speak Joan's name. One's voice would have broken down. We knew who was meant when she was mentioned; we could say "she" and "her," but we could not speak the name.

We talked of the personal staff. Old D'Aulon, wounded and a prisoner, was still with Joan and serving her, by permission of the Duke of Burgundy. Joan was being treated with the respect due to her rank and to her character as a prisoner of war taken in honorable conflict. And this was continued — as we learned later — until she fell into the hands of that bastard of Satan, Pierre Cauchon, Bishop of Beauvais.

Noël was full of noble and affectionate praises and appreciations of our old boastful big Standard-Bearer, now gone silent forever, his real and imaginary battles all fought, his work done, his life honorably closed and completed.

"And think of his luck!" burst out Noël, with his eyes full of tears. "Always the pet child of luck! See how it followed him and stayed by him, from his first step all through, in the field or out of it; always a splendid figure in the public eye, courted and envied everywhere; always having a chance to do fine things and always doing them; in the beginning called the Paladin in joke, and called it afterward in earnest because he magnificently made the title good; and at last — supremest luck of all — died in the field! died with his harness on; died faithful to his charge, the Standard in his hand; died — oh, think of it — with the approving eye of

Joan of Arc upon him! He drained the cup of glory to the last drop, and went jubilant to his peace, blessedly spared all part in the disaster which was to follow. What luck, what luck! And we? What was our sin that we are still here, we who have also earned our place with the happy dead?"

And presently he said:

"They tore the sacred Standard from his dead hand and carried it away, their most precious prize after its captured owner. But they haven't it now. A month ago we put our lives upon the risk—our two good knights, my fellow-prisoners, and I—and stole it, and got it smuggled by trusty hands to Orleans, and there it is now, safe for all time in the Treasury."

I was glad and grateful to learn that. I have seen it often since, when I have gone to Orleans on the 8th of May to be the petted old guest of the city and hold the first place of honor at the banquets and in the processions—I mean since Joan's brothers passed from this life. It will still be there, sacredly guarded by French love, a thousand years from now—yes, as long as any shred of it hangs together.*

* It remained there three hundred and sixty years, and then was destroyed in a public bonfire, together with two swords, a plumed çap, several suits of state apparel, and other relics of the Maid, by a mob in the time of the Revolution. Nothing which the hand of Joan of Arc is known to have touched now remains in existence except a few preciously guarded military and state papers which she signed, her pen being guided by a clerk or her secretary Louis de Conte. A bowlder exists

Two or three weeks after this talk came the tremendous news like a thunder-clap, and we were aghast — Joan of Arc sold to the English!

Not for a moment had we ever dreamed of such a thing. We were young, you see, and did not know the human race, as I have said before. We had been so proud of our country, so sure of her nobleness, her magnanimity, her gratitude. We had expected little of the King, but of France we had expected everything. Everybody knew that in various towns patriot priests had been marching in procession urging the people to sacrifice money, property, everything, and buy the freedom of their heaven-sent deliverer. That the money would be raised we had not thought of doubting.

But it was all over now, all over. It was a bitter time for us. The heavens seemed hung with black; all cheer went out from our hearts. Was this comrade here at my bedside really Noël Rainguesson, that light-hearted creature whose whole life was but one long joke, and who used up more breath in laughter than in keeping his body alive? No, no; *that* Noël I was to see no more. This one's heart was broken. He moved grieving about, and ab-

---

from which she is known to have mounted her horse when she was once setting out upon a campaign. Up to a quarter of a century ago there was a single hair from her head still in existence. It was drawn through the wax of a seal attached to the parchment of a state document. It was surreptitiously snipped out, seal and all, by some vandal relic-hunter, and carried off. Doubtless it still exists, but only the thief knows where.—TRANSLATOR.

sently, like one in a dream; the stream of his laughter was dried at its source.

Well, that was best. It was my own mood. We were company for each other. He nursed me patiently through the dull long weeks, and at last, in January, I was strong enough to go about again. Then he said:

"Shall we go now?"

"Yes."

There was no need to explain. Our hearts were in Rouen; we would carry our bodies there. All that we cared for in this life was shut up in that fortress. We could not help her, but it would be some solace to us to be near her, to breathe the air that she breathed, and look daily upon the stone walls that hid her. What if we should be made prisoners there? Well, we could but do our best, and let luck and fate decide what should happen.

And so we started. We could not realize the change which had come upon the country. We seemed able to choose our own route and go wherever we pleased, unchallenged and unmolested. When Joan of Arc was in the field, there was a sort of panic of fear everywhere; but now that she was out of the way, fear had vanished. Nobody was troubled about you or afraid of you, nobody was curious about you or your business, everybody was indifferent.

We presently saw that we could take to the Seine, and not weary ourselves out with land travel. So we did it, and were carried in a boat to within a league of Rouen. Then we got ashore; not on the hilly side, but on the other, where it is as level as a floor. Nobody could enter or leave the city without explaining himself. It was because they feared attempts at a rescue of Joan.

We had no trouble. We stopped in the plain with a family of peasants and stayed a week, helping them with their work for board and lodging, and making friends of them. We got clothes like theirs, and wore them. When we had worked our way through their reserves and gotten their confidence, we found that they secretly harbored French hearts in their bodies. Then we came out frankly and told them everything, and found them ready to do anything they could to help us. Our plan was soon made, and was quite simple. It was to help them drive a flock of sheep to the market of the city. One morning early we made the venture in a melancholy drizzle of rain, and passed through the frowning gates unmolested. Our friends had friends living over a humble wine-shop in a quaint tall building situated in one of the narrow lanes that run down from the cathedral to the river, and with these they bestowed us; and the next day they smuggled our own proper clothing and other belongings to us. The family that lodged us — the Pierrons — were French in sympathy, and we needed to have no secrets from them.

CHAPTER III.

IT was necessary for me to have some way to gain bread for Noël and myself; and when the Pierrons found that I knew how to write, they applied to their confessor in my behalf, and he got a place for me with a good priest named Manchon, who was to be the chief recorder in the Great Trial of Joan of Arc now approaching. It was a strange position for me — clerk to the recorder — and dangerous if my sympathies and late employment should be found out. But there was not much danger. Manchon was at bottom friendly to Joan and would not betray me; and my name would not, for I had discarded my surname and retained only my given one, like a person of low degree.

I attended Manchon constantly straight along, out of January and into February, and was often in the citadel with him — in the very fortress where Joan was imprisoned, though not in the dungeon where she was confined, and so did not see her, of course.

Manchon told me everything that had been happening before my coming. Ever since the purchase of Joan, Cauchon had been busy packing his jury for the destruction of the Maid — weeks and weeks he had spent in this bad industry. The University of Paris had sent him a number of learned and able and trusty ecclesiastics of the stripe he wanted; and he had scraped together a clergyman of like stripe and great fame here and there and yonder, until he was able to construct a formidable court numbering half a hundred distinguished names. French names they were, but their interests and sympathies were English.

A great officer of the Inquisition was also sent from Paris, for the accused must be tried by the forms of the Inquisition; but this was a brave and righteous man, and he said squarely that this court had no power to try the case, wherefore he refused to act; and the same honest talk was uttered by two or three others.

The Inquisitor was right. The case as here resurrected against Joan had already been tried long ago at Poitiers, and decided in her favor. Yes, and by a higher tribunal than this one, for at the head of it was an Archbishop — he of Rheims — Cauchon's own metropolitan. So here, you see, a lower court was impudently preparing to re-try and re-decide a cause which had already been decided by its superior, a court of higher authority. Imagine it! No, the case could not properly be tried again. Cauchon could not properly preside in this new court, for more than one reason: Rouen was not in his diocese; Joan had not been arrested in her domicile, which was still Domremy; and finally this proposed judge was the prisoner's outspoken enemy, and therefore he was incompetent to try her. Yet all these large difficulties were gotten rid of. The territorial Chapter of Rouen finally granted territorial letters to Cauchon — though only after a struggle and under compulsion. Force was also applied to the Inquisitor, and he was obliged to submit.

So, then, the little English King, by his representative, formally delivered Joan into the hands of the court, but with this reservation: *if the court failed to condemn her, he was to have her back again!*

Ah, dear, what chance was there for that forsaken and friendless child? Friendless, indeed — it is the right word. For she was in a black dungeon, with half a dozen brutal common soldiers keeping guard night and day in the room where her cage was — for she was in a cage; an iron cage, and chained to her bed by neck and hands and feet. Never a person near her whom she had ever seen before; never a woman at all. Yes, this was, indeed, friendlessness.

Now it was a vassal of Jean de Luxembourg who captured Joan at Compiègne, and it was Jean who sold her to the Duke of Burgundy. Yet this very De Luxembourg was shameless enough to go and show his face to Joan in her cage. He came with two English earls, Warwick and Stafford. He was a poor reptile. He told her he would get her set free if she would promise not to fight the English any more. She had been in that cage a long time now, but not long enough to break her spirit. She retorted scornfully:

"Name of God, you but mock me. I know that you have neither the power nor the will to do it."

He insisted. Then the pride and dignity of the soldier rose in Joan, and she lifted her chained hands and let them fall with a clash, saying:

"See these! They know more than you, and can prophesy better. I know that the English are going to kill me, for they think that when I am dead they can get the Kingdom of France. It is not so. Though there were a hundred thousand of them they would never get it."

This defiance infuriated Stafford, and he—now think of it—he a free, strong man, she a chained and helpless girl—he drew his dagger and flung himself at her to stab her. But Warwick seized him and held him back. Warwick was wise. Take her life in that way? Send her to Heaven stainless and undisgraced? It would make her the idol of France, and the whole nation would rise and march to victory and emancipation under the inspiration of her spirit. No, she must be saved for another fate than that.

Well, the time was approaching for the Great Trial. For more than two months Cauchon had been raking and scraping everywhere for any odds and ends of evidence or suspicion or conjecture that might be made usable against Joan, and carefully suppressing all evidence that came to hand in her favor. He had limitless ways and means and powers at his disposal for preparing and strengthening the case for the prosecution, and he used them all.

But Joan had no one to prepare her case for her, and she was shut up in those stone walls and had no friend to appeal to for help. And as for witnesses, she could not call a single one in her defense; they were all far away, under the French flag, and this was an English court; they would have been seized and hanged if they had shown their faces at the gates of Rouen. No, the prisoner must be the *sole* witness — witness for the prosecution, witness for the defense; and with a verdict of death resolved upon before the doors were opened for the court's first sitting.

When she learned that the court was made up of ecclesiastics in the interest of the English, she begged that in fairness an equal number of priests of the French party should be added to these. Cauchon scoffed at her message, and would not even deign to answer it.

By the law of the Church — she being a minor under twenty-one — it was her right to have counsel to conduct her case, advise her how to answer when questioned, and protect her from falling into traps set by cunning devices of the prosecution. She probably did not know that this was her right, and that she could demand it and require it, for there was none to tell her that; but she begged for this help at any rate. Cauchon refused it. She urged and implored, pleading her youth and her ignorance of the complexities and intricacies of the law and of legal procedure. Cauchon refused again, and said she must get along with her case as best she might by herself. Ah, his heart was a stone.

Cauchon prepared the *proces verbal.* I will simplify that by calling it the Bill of Particulars. It was a detailed list of the charges against her, and formed the basis of the trial. Charges? It was a list of *suspicions and public rumors* — those were the words used. It was merely charged that she was suspected of having been guilty of heresies, witchcraft, and other such offenses against religion.

Now by law of the Church, a trial of that sort could not be begun until a searching inquiry had been made into the history and character of the accused, and it was essential that the result of this inquiry be added to the *proces verbal* and form a part of it. You remember that that was the first thing they did before the trial at Poitiers. They did it again now. An ecclesiastic was sent to Domremy. There and all about the neighborhood he made an exhaustive search into Joan's history and character, and came back with his verdict. It was very clear. The searcher reported that he found Joan's character to be in every way what he "would like his own sister's character to be." Just about the same report that was brought back to Poitiers, you see. Joan's was a character which could endure the minutest examination.

This verdict was a strong point for Joan, you will say. Yes, it *would* have been if it could have seen the light; but Cauchon was awake, and it disappeared from the *proces verbal* before the trial. People were prudent enough not to inquire what became of it.

One would imagine that Cauchon was ready to begin the trial by this time. But no, he devised one more scheme for poor Joan's destruction, and it promised to be a deadly one.

One of the great personages picked out and sent down by the University of Paris was an ecclesiastic named Nicolas Loyseleur. He was tall, handsome, grave, of smooth soft speech and courteous and winning manners. There was no seeming of treachery or hypocrisy about him, yet he was full of both. He was admitted to Joan's prison by night, disguised as a cobbler; he pretended to be from her own country; he professed to be secretly a patriot; he revealed the fact that he was a priest. She was filled with gladness to see one from the hills and plains that were so dear to her; happier still to look upon a priest and disburden her heart in confession, for the offices of the Church were the bread of life, the breath of her nostrils to her, and she had been long forced to pine for them in vain. She opened her whole innocent heart to this creature, and in return he gave her advice concerning her trial which could have destroyed her if her deep native wisdom had not protected her against following it.

You will ask, what value could this scheme have, since the secrets of the confessional are sacred and cannot be revealed? True — but suppose another person should overhear them? That person is not bound to keep the secret. Well, that is what happened. Cauchon had previously caused a hole to be bored through the wall; and he stood with his ear to that hole and heard all. It is pitiful to think of these things. One wonders how they could treat that poor child so. She had not done them any harm.

CHAPTER IV.

ON Tuesday, the 20th of February, while I sat at my master's work in the evening, he came in, looking sad, and said it had been decided to begin the trial at eight o'clock the next morning, and I must get ready to assist him.

Of course I had been expecting such news every day for many days; but no matter, the shock of it almost took my breath away and set me trembling like a leaf. I suppose that without knowing it I had been half imagining that at the last moment something would happen, something that would stop this fatal trial: maybe that La Hire would burst in at the gates with his hellions at his back; maybe that God would have pity and stretch forth His mighty hand. But now—now there was no hope.

The trial was to begin in the chapel of the fortress and would be public. So I went sorrowing away and told Noël, so that he might be there early and secure a place. It would give him a chance to look again upon the face which we so revered and which was so precious to us. All the way, both going and coming, I plowed through chattering and rejoicing multitudes of English soldiery and English-hearted French citizens. There was no talk but of the coming event. Many times I heard the remark, accompanied by a pitiless laugh:

"The fat Bishop has got things as he wants them at last, and says he will lead the vile witch a merry dance and a short one."

But here and there I glimpsed compassion and distress in a face, and it was not always a French one. English soldiers feared Joan, but they admired her for her great deeds and her unconquerable spirit.

In the morning Manchon and I went early, yet as we approached the vast fortress we found crowds of men already there and still others gathering. The chapel was already full and the way barred against further admissions of unofficial persons. We took our appointed places. Throned on high sat the president, Cauchon, Bishop of Beauvais, in his grand robes, and before him in rows sat his robed court—fifty distinguished ecclesiastics, men of high degree in the Church, of clear-cut intellectual faces, men of deep learning, veteran adepts in strategy and casuistry, practiced setters of traps for ignorant minds and unwary feet. When I looked around upon this army of masters of legal fence, gathered here to find just one verdict and no other, and remembered that Joan must fight for her good name and her life single-handed against them, I asked myself what chance an ignorant poor country girl of nineteen could have in such an unequal conflict; and my heart sank down low, very low. When I looked again at that obese president, puffing and wheezing there, his great belly distending and receding with each breath, and noted his three chins, fold above fold, and his knobby and knotty face, and his purple and splotchy complexion, and his repulsive cauliflower nose, and his cold and malignant eyes — a brute, every detail of him — my heart sank lower still. And when I noted that all were afraid of this man, and shrank and fidgeted in their seats when his eye smote theirs, my last poor ray of hope dissolved away and wholly disappeared.

There was one unoccupied seat in this place, and only one. It was over against the wall, in view of every one. It was a little wooden bench without a back, and it stood apart and solitary on a sort of dais. Tall men-at-arms in morion, breastplate, and steel gauntlets stood as stiff as their own halberds on each side of this dais, but no other creature was near by it. A pathetic little bench to me it was, for I knew whom it was for; and the sight of it carried my mind back to the great court at Poitiers, where Joan sat upon one like it and calmly fought her cunning fight with the astonished doctors of the Church and Parliament, and rose from it victorious and applauded by all, and went forth to fill the world with the glory of her name.

What a dainty little figure she was, and how gentle and innocent, how winning and beautiful in the fresh bloom of her seventeen years! Those were grand days. And so recent — for she was but just nineteen now — and how much she had seen since, and what wonders she had accomplished!

But now — oh, all was changed now. She had been languishing in dungeons, away from light and air and the cheer of friendly faces, for nearly three-quarters of a year — she, born child of the sun, natural comrade of the birds and of all happy free creatures. She would be weary now, and worn with this long captivity, her forces impaired; despondent, perhaps, as knowing there was no hope. Yes, all was changed.

All this time there had been a muffled hum of conversation, and rustling of robes and scraping of feet on the floor, a combination of dull noises which filled all the place. Suddenly:

"Produce the accused!"

It made me catch my breath. My heart began to thump like a hammer. But there was silence now — silence absolute. All those noises ceased, and it was as if they had never been. Not a sound; the stillness grew oppressive; it was like a weight upon one. All faces were turned toward the door; and one could properly expect that, for most of the people there suddenly realized, no doubt, that they were about to see, in actual flesh and blood, what had been to them before only an embodied prodigy, a word, a phrase, a world-girdling Name.

The stillness continued. Then, far down the

stone-paved corridors, one heard a vague slow sound approaching: *clank*. . . . . .clink. . . . . .clank — Joan of Arc, Deliverer of France, in chains!

My head swam; all things whirled and spun about me. Ah, *I* was realizing, too.

CHAPTER V.

I GIVE you my honor now that I am not going to distort or discolor the facts of this miserable trial. No, I will give them to you honestly, detail by detail, just as Manchon and I set them down daily in the official record of the court, and just as one may read them in the printed histories. There will be only this difference: that in talking familiarly with you I shall use my right to comment upon the proceedings and explain them as I go along, so that you can understand them better; also, I shall throw in trifles which came under our eyes and have a certain interest for you and me, but were not important enough to go into the official record.*

To take up my story now where I left off. We heard the clanking of Joan's chains down the corridors; she was approaching.

Presently she appeared; a thrill swept the house, and one heard deep breaths drawn. Two guardsmen followed her at a short distance to the rear. Her

* He kept his word. His account of the Great Trial will be found to be in strict and detailed accordance with the sworn facts of history.—TRANSLATOR.

head was bowed a little, and she moved slowly, she being weak and her irons heavy. She had on men's attire — all black; a soft woolen stuff, intensely black, funereally black, not a speck of relieving color in it from her throat to the floor. A wide collar of this same black stuff lay in radiating folds upon her shoulders and breast; the sleeves of her doublet were full, down to the elbows, and tight thence to her manacled wrists; below the doublet, tight black hose down to the chains on her ankles.

Half way to her bench she stopped, just where a wide shaft of light fell slanting from a window, and slowly lifted her face. Another thrill! — it was totally colorless, white as snow; a face of gleaming snow set in vivid contrast upon that slender statue of somber unmitigated black. It was smooth and pure and girlish, beautiful beyond belief, infinitely sad and sweet. But, dear, dear! when the challenge of those untamed eyes fell upon that judge, and the droop vanished from her form and it straightened up soldierly and noble, my heart leaped for joy; and I said, all is well, all is well — they have not broken her, they have not conquered her, she is Joan of Arc still! Yes, it was plain to me now that there was one spirit there which this dreaded judge could not quell nor make afraid.

She moved to her place and mounted the dais and seated herself upon her bench, gathering her chains into her lap and nestling her little white hands there. Then she waited in tranquil dignity, the only person there who seemed unmoved and unexcited. A bronzed and brawny English soldier, standing at martial ease in the front rank of the citizen spectators, did now most gallantly and respectfully put up his great hand and give her the military salute; and she, smiling friendly, put up hers and returned it; whereat there was a sympathetic little break of applause, which the judge sternly silenced.

Now the memorable inquisition called in history the Great Trial began. Fifty experts against a novice, and no one to help the novice!

The judge summarized the circumstances of the case and the public reports and suspicions upon which it was based; then he required Joan to kneel and make oath that she would answer with exact truthfulness to all questions asked her.

Joan's mind was not asleep. It suspected that dangerous possibilities might lie hidden under this apparently fair and reasonable demand. She answered with the simplicity which so often spoiled the enemy's best-laid plans in the trial at Poitiers, and said:

"No; for I do not know what you are going to ask me; you might ask of me things which I would not tell you."

This incensed the Court, and brought out a brisk flurry of angry exclamations. Joan was not disturbed. Cauchon raised his voice and began to speak in the midst of this noise, but he was so angry that he could hardly get his words out. He said:

"With the divine assistance of our Lord we require you to expedite these proceedings for the welfare of your conscience. Swear, with your hands upon the Gospels, that you will answer true to the questions which shall be asked you!" and he brought down his fat hand with a crash upon his official table.

Joan said, with composure:

"As concerning my father and mother, and the faith, and what things I have done since my coming into France, I will gladly answer; but as regards the revelations which I have received from God, my Voices have forbidden me to confide them to any save my King—"

Here there was another angry outburst of threats and expletives, and much movement and confusion; so she had to stop, and wait for the noise to subside; then her waxen face flushed a little and she straightened up and fixed her eye on the judge, and finished her sentence in a voice that had the old ring in it:

"—and I will never reveal these things though you cut my head off!"

Well, maybe you know what a deliberative body of Frenchmen is like. The judge and half the court were on their feet in a moment, and all shaking their fists at the prisoner, and all storming and vituperating at once, so that you could hardly hear yourself think. They kept this up several minutes; and because Joan sat untroubled and indifferent, they grew madder and noisier all the time. Once she said, with a fleeting trace of the old-time mischief in her eye and manner:

"Prithee, speak one at a time, fair lords, then I will answer all of you."

At the end of three whole hours of furious debating over the oath, the situation had not changed a jot. The Bishop was still requiring an unmodified oath, Joan was refusing for the twentieth time to take any except the one which she had herself proposed. There was a physical change apparent, but it was confined to court and judge; they were hoarse, droopy, exhausted by their long frenzy, and had a sort of haggard look in their faces, poor men, whereas Joan was still placid and reposeful and did not seem noticeably tired.

The noise quieted down; there was a waiting pause of some moments' duration. Then the judge surrendered to the prisoner, and with bitterness in his voice told her to take the oath after her own fashion. Joan sunk at once to her knees; and as she laid her hands upon the Gospels, that big English soldier set free his mind:

"By God, if she were but English, she were not in this place another half a second!"

It was the soldier in him responding to the soldier in her. But what a stinging rebuke it was, what an arraignment of French character and French royalty! Would that he could have uttered just that one phrase in the hearing of Orleans! I know that that

THE TRIAL OF JOAN OF ARC

grateful city, that adoring city, would have risen, to the last man and the last woman, and marched upon Rouen. Some speeches—speeches that shame a man and humble him—burn themselves into the memory and remain there. That one is burned into mine.

After Joan had made oath, Cauchon asked her her name, and where she was born, and some questions about her family; also what her age was. She answered these. Then he asked her how much education she had.

"I have learned from my mother the Pater Noster, the Ave Maria, and the Belief. All that I know was taught me by my mother."

Questions of this unessential sort dribbled on for a considerable time. Everybody was tired out by now, except Joan. The tribunal prepared to rise. At this point Cauchon forbade Joan to try to escape from prison, upon pain of being held guilty of the crime of heresy—singular logic! She answered simply:

"I am not bound by this prohibition. If I could escape I would not reproach myself, for I have given no promise, and I shall not."

Then she complained of the burden of her chains, and asked that they might be removed, for she was strongly guarded in that dungeon and there was no need of them. But the Bishop refused, and reminded her that she had broken out of prison twice before. Joan of Arc was too proud to insist. She only said, as she rose to go with the guard:

"It is true I have wanted to escape, and I do want to escape." Then she added, in a way that would touch the pity of anybody, I think, "It is the right of every prisoner."

And so she went from the place in the midst of an impressive stillness, which made the sharper and more distressful to me the clank of those pathetic chains.

What presence of mind she had! One could never surprise her out of it. She saw Noël and me there when she first took her seat on her bench, and we flushed to the forehead with excitement and emotion, but her face showed nothing, betrayed nothing. Her eyes sought us fifty times that day, but they passed on and there was never any ray of recognition in them. Another would have started upon seeing us, and then — why then there could have been trouble for us, of course.

We walked slowly home together, each busy with his own grief and saying not a word.

CHAPTER VI.

THAT night Manchon told me that all through the day's proceedings Cauchon had had some clerks concealed in the embrasure of a window who were to make a special report garbling Joan's answers and twisting them from their right meaning. Ah, that was surely the cruelest man and the most shameless that has lived in this world. But his scheme failed. Those clerks had human hearts in them, and their base work revolted them, and they turned to and boldly made a straight report, whereupon Cauchon cursed them and ordered them out of his presence with a threat of drowning, which was his favorite and most frequent menace. The matter had gotten abroad and was making great and unpleasant talk, and Cauchon would not try to repeat this shabby game right away. It comforted me to hear that.

When we arrived at the citadel next morning, we found that a change had been made. The chapel had been found too small. The court had now removed to a noble chamber situated at the end of the great hall of the castle. The number of judges was increased to sixty-two — one ignorant girl against such odds, and none to help her.

The prisoner was brought in. She was as white as ever, but she was looking no whit worse than she looked when she had first appeared the day before. Isn't it a strange thing? Yesterday she had sat five hours on that backless bench with her chains in her lap, baited, badgered, persecuted by that unholy crew, without even the refreshment of a cup of water — for she was never offered anything, and if I have made you know her by this time you will know without my telling you that she was not a person likely to ask favors of those people. And she had spent the night caged in her wintry dungeon with her chains upon her; yet here she was, as I say, collected, unworn, and ready for the conflict; yes, and the only person there who showed no signs of the wear and worry of yesterday. And her eyes — ah, you should have seen them and broken your hearts. Have you seen that veiled deep glow, that pathetic hurt dignity, that unsubdued and unsubduable spirit that burns and smoulders in the eye of a caged eagle and makes you feel mean and shabby under the burden of its mute reproach? Her eyes were like that. How capable they were, and how wonderful! Yes, at all times and in all circumstances they could express as by print every shade of the wide range of her moods. In them were hidden floods of gay sunshine, the softest and peacefulest twilights, and devastating storms and lightnings.

Not in this world have there been others that were comparable to them. Such is my opinion, and none that had the privilege to see them would say otherwise than this which I have said concerning them.

The seance began. And how did it begin, should you think? Exactly as it began before — with that same tedious thing which had been settled once, after so much wrangling. The Bishop opened thus:

"You are required, now, to take the oath pure and simple, to answer truly all questions asked you."

Joan replied placidly:

"I have made oath yesterday, my lord; let that suffice."

The Bishop insisted and insisted, with rising temper; Joan but shook her head and remained silent. At last she said:

"I made oath yesterday; it is sufficient." Then she sighed and said, "Of a truth, you do burden me too much."

The Bishop still insisted, still commanded, but he could not move her. At last he gave it up and turned her over for the day's inquest to an old hand at tricks and traps and deceptive plausibilities — Beaupere, a doctor of theology. Now notice the form of this sleek strategist's first remark — flung out in an easy, off-hand way that would have thrown any unwatchful person off his guard:

"Now, Joan, the matter is very simple; just

speak up and frankly and truly answer the questions which I am going to ask you, as you have sworn to do."

It was a failure. Joan was not asleep. She saw the artifice. She said:

"No. You could ask me things which I could not tell you—and would not." Then, reflecting upon how profane and out of character it was for these ministers of God to be prying into matters which had proceeded from His hands under the awful seal of His secrecy, she added, with a warning note in her tone, "If you were well informed concerning me you would wish me out of your hands. I have done nothing but by revelation."

Beaupere changed his attack, and began an approach from another quarter. He would slip upon her, you see, under cover of innocent and unimportant questions.

"Did you learn any trade at home?"

"Yes, to sew and to spin." Then the invincible soldier, victor of Patay, conqueror of the lion Talbot, deliverer of Orleans, restorer of a king's crown, commander-in-chief of a nation's armies, straightened herself proudly up, gave her head a little toss, and said with naïve complacency, "And when it comes to that, I am not afraid to be matched against any woman in Rouen!"

The crowd of spectators broke out with applause—which pleased Joan—and there was many a friendly and petting smile to be seen. But Cauchon stormed at the people and warned them to keep still and mind their manners.

Beaupere asked other questions. Then:

"Had you other occupations at home?"

"Yes. I helped my mother in the household work and went to the pastures with the sheep and the cattle."

Her voice trembled a little, but one could hardly notice it. As for me, it brought those old enchanted days flooding back to me, and I could not see what I was writing for a little while.

Beaupere cautiously edged along up with other questions toward the forbidden ground, and finally repeated a question which she had refused to answer a little while back—as to whether she had received the Eucharist in those days at other festivals than that of Easter. Joan merely said:

"*Passez outre.*" Or, as one might say, "Pass on to matters which you are privileged to pry into."

I heard a member of the court say to a neighbor:

"As a rule, witnesses are but dull creatures, and an easy prey—yes, and easily embarrassed, easily frightened—but truly one can neither scare this child nor find her dozing."

Presently the house pricked up its ears and began to listen eagerly, for Beaupere began to touch upon Joan's Voices, a matter of consuming interest and curiosity to everybody. His purpose was, to trick her into heedless sayings that could indicate that the Voices had sometimes given her evil advice—hence that they had come from Satan, you see. To have dealings with the devil — well, that would send her to the stake in brief order, and that was the deliberate end and aim of this trial.

"When did you first hear these Voices?"

"I was thirteen when I first heard a Voice coming from God to help me to live well. I was frightened. It came at mid-day, in my father's garden in the summer."

"Had you been fasting?"

"Yes."

"The day before?"

"No."

"From what direction did it come?"

"From the right — from toward the church."

"Did it come with a bright light?"

"Oh, indeed yes. It was brilliant. When I came into France I often heard the Voices very loud."

"What did the Voice sound like?"

"It was a noble Voice, and I thought it was sent to me from God. The third time I heard it I recognized it as being an angel's."

"You could understand it?"

"Quite easily. It was always clear."

"What advice did it give you as to the salvation of your soul?"

"It told me to live rightly, and be regular in attendance upon the services of the Church. And it told me that I must go to France."

"In what species of form did the Voice appear?"

Joan looked suspiciously at the priest a moment, then said, tranquilly:

"As to that, I will not tell you."

"Did the Voice seek you often?"

"Yes. Twice or three times a week, saying, 'Leave your village and go to France.'"

"Did your father know about your departure?"

"No. The Voice said, 'Go to France'; therefore I could not abide at home any longer."

"What else did it say?"

"That I should raise the siege of Orleans."

"Was that all?"

"No, I was to go to Vaucouleurs, and Robert de Baudricourt would give me soldiers to go with me to France; and I answered, saying that I was a poor girl who did not know how to ride, neither how to fight."

Then she told how she was balked and interrupted at Vaucouleurs, but finally got her soldiers, and began her march.

"How were you dressed?"

The court of Poitiers had distinctly decided and decreed that as God had appointed her to do a man's work, it was meet and no scandal to religion that she should dress as a man; but no matter, this court was ready to use any and all weapons against Joan, even broken and discredited ones, and much was going to be made of this one before this trial should end.

"I wore a man's dress, also a sword which Robert de Baudricourt gave me, but no other weapon."

"Who was it that advised you to wear the dress of a man?"

Joan was suspicious again. She would not answer.

The question was repeated.

She refused again.

"Answer. It is a command!"

"*Passez outre*," was all she said.

So Beaupere gave up the matter for the present.

"What did Baudricourt say to you when you left?"

"He made them that were to go with me promise to take charge of me, and to me he said, 'Go, and let happen what may!'" (*Advienne que pourra!*)

After a good deal of questioning upon other matters she was asked again about her attire. She said it was necessary for her to dress as a man.

"Did your Voice advise it?"

Joan merely answered placidly:

"I believe my Voice gave me good advice."

It was all that could be got out of her, so the questions wandered to other matters, and finally to her first meeting with the King at Chinon. She said she chose out the King, who was unknown to her, by the revelation of her Voices. All that happened at that time was gone over. Finally:

"Do you still hear those Voices?"

"They come to me every day."

"What do you ask of them?"

"I have never asked of them any recompense but the salvation of my soul."

"Did the Voice always urge you to follow the army?"

He is creeping upon her again. She answered:

"It required me to remain behind at St. Denis. I would have obeyed if I had been free, but I was helpless by my wound, and the knights carried me away by force."

"When were you wounded?"

"I was wounded in the moat before Paris, in the assault."

The next question reveals what Beaupere had been leading up to:

"Was it a feast day?"

You see? The suggestion is that a voice coming from God would hardly advise or permit the violation, by war and bloodshed, of a sacred day.

Joan was troubled a moment, then she answered yes, it was a feast day.

"Now, then, tell me this: did you hold it right to make the attack on such a day?"

This was a shot which might make the first breach in a wall which had suffered no damage thus far. There was immediate silence in the court and intense expectancy noticeable all about. But Joan disappointed the house. She merely made a slight little motion with her hand, as when one brushes away a fly, and said with reposeful indifference:

"*Passez outre.*"

Smiles danced for a moment in some of the sternest faces there, and several even laughed outright. The trap had been long and laboriously prepared; it fell, and was empty.

The court rose. It had sat for hours, and was cruelly fatigued. Most of the time had been taken up with apparently idle and purposeless inquiries about the Chinon events, the exiled Duke of Orleans, Joan's first proclamation, and so on, but all this seemingly random stuff had really been sown thick with hidden traps. But Joan had fortunately escaped them all, some by the protecting luck which attends upon ignorance and innocence, some by happy accident, the others by force of her best and surest helper, the clear vision and lightning intuitions of her extraordinary mind.

Now, then, this daily baiting and badgering of this friendless girl, a captive in chains, was to continue a long, long time—dignified sport, a kennel of mastiffs and bloodhounds harassing a kitten!—and I may as well tell you, upon sworn testimony, what it was like from the first day to the last. When poor Joan had been in her grave a quarter of a century, the Pope called together that great court which was to re-examine her history, and whose just verdict cleared her illustrious name from every spot and stain, and laid upon the verdict and conduct of our Rouen tribunal the blight of its everlasting execrations. Manchon and several of the judges who had been members of our court were among the witnesses who appeared before that Tribunal of Rehabilitation. Recalling these miserable proceedings which I have been telling you about, Manchon testified thus: — here you have it, all in fair print in the official history:

> When Joan spoke of her apparitions she was interrupted at almost every word. They wearied her with long and multiplied interrogatories upon all sorts of things. Almost every day the interrogatories of the morning lasted *three or four hours;* then from these morning-interrogatories they extracted the particularly difficult and subtle points, and these served as material for the afternoon-interrogatories, which lasted *two or three hours.* Moment by moment they skipped from one subject to another; yet in spite of this *she always responded with an astonishing wisdom and memory.* She often corrected the judges, saying, "But I have already answered that once before — ask the recorder," referring them to me.

And here is the testimony of one of Joan's judges. Remember, these witnesses are not talking about two or three days, they are talking about a tedious long *procession* of days:

> They asked her profound questions, but she extricated herself quite well. Sometimes the questioners changed suddenly and passed to another subject *to see if she would not contradict herself.* They burdened her with long interrogatories of two or three hours, from which *the judges themselves went forth fatigued.* From the snares with which she was beset *the expertest man in the world could not have extricated himself but with difficulty.* She gave her responses with great prudence; indeed to such a degree that during *three weeks I believed she was inspired.*

Ah, had she a mind such as I have described? You see what these priests say under oath — picked men, men chosen for their places in that terrible court on account of their learning, their experience, their keen and practiced intellects, and their strong bias against the prisoner. They make that poor young country girl out the match, and more than the match, of the sixty-two trained adepts. Isn't it so? They from the University of Paris, she from the sheepfold and the cow-stable! Ah, yes, she was great, she was wonderful. It took six thousand years to produce her; her like will not be seen in the earth again in fifty thousand. Such is my opinion.

CHAPTER VII.

THE third meeting of the court was in that same spacious chamber, next day, 24th of February. How did it begin work? In just the same old way. When the preparations were ended, the robed sixty-two massed in their chairs and the guards and order-keepers distributed to their stations, Cauchon spoke from his throne and commanded Joan to lay her hands upon the Gospels and swear to tell the truth concerning everything asked her!

Joan's eyes kindled, and she rose; rose and stood, fine and noble, and faced toward the Bishop and said:

"Take care what you do, my Lord, you who are my judge, for you take a terrible responsibility on yourself and you presume too far."

It made a great stir, and Cauchon burst out upon her with an awful threat — the threat of instant condemnation unless she obeyed. That made the very bones in my body turn cold, and I saw cheeks about me blanch — for it meant fire and the stake! But Joan, still standing, answered him back, proud and undismayed:

"Not all the clergy in Paris and Rouen could condemn me, lacking the right!"

This made a great tumult, and part of it was applause from the spectators. Joan resumed her seat. The Bishop still insisted. Joan said:

"I have already made oath. It is enough."

The Bishop shouted:

"In refusing to swear, you place yourself under suspicion!"

"Let be. I have sworn already. It is enough."

The Bishop continued to insist. Joan answered that "she would tell what she knew—but not all that she knew."

The Bishop plagued her straight along, till at last she said, in a weary tone:

"I came from God; I have nothing more to do here. Return me to God, from whom I came."

It was piteous to hear; it was the same as saying, "You only want my life; take it and let me be at peace."

The Bishop stormed out again:

"Once more I command you to—"

Joan cut in with a nonchalant "*Passez outre*," and Cauchon retired from the struggle; but he retired with some credit this time, for he offered a compromise, and Joan, always clear-headed, saw protection for herself in it and promptly and willingly accepted it. She was to swear to tell the truth "as touching the matters set down in the *proces verbal.*" They could not sail her outside of definite limits, now;

her course was over a charted sea, henceforth. The Bishop had granted more than he had intended, and more than he would honestly try to abide by.

By command, Beaupere resumed his examination of the accused. It being Lent, there might be a chance to catch her neglecting some detail of her religious duties. I could have told him he would fail there. Why, religion was her life!

"Since when have you eaten or drunk?"

If the least thing had passed her lips in the nature of sustenance, neither her youth nor the fact that she was being half starved in her prison could save her from dangerous suspicion of contempt for the commandments of the Church.

"I have done neither since yesterday at noon."

The priest shifted to the Voices again.

"When have you heard your Voice?"

"Yesterday and to-day."

"At what time?"

"Yesterday it was in the morning."

"What were you doing then?"

"I was asleep and it woke me."

"By touching your arm?"

"No; without touching me."

"Did you thank it? Did you kneel?"

He had Satan in his mind, you see; and was hoping, perhaps, that by and by it could be shown that she had rendered homage to the arch enemy of God and man.

"Yes, I thanked it; and knelt in my bed where I

was chained, and joined my hands and begged it to implore God's help for me so that I might have light and instruction as touching the answers I should give here."

"Then what did the Voice say?"

"It told me to answer boldly, and God would help me." Then she turned toward Cauchon and said, "You say that you are my judge; now I tell you again, take care what you do, for in truth I am sent of God and you are putting yourself in great danger."

Beaupere asked her if the Voice's counsels were not fickle and variable.

"No. It never contradicts itself. This very day it has told me again to answer boldly."

"Has it forbidden you to answer only part of what is asked you?"

"I will tell you nothing as to that. I have revelations touching the King my master, and those I will not tell you." Then she was stirred by a great emotion, and the tears sprang to her eyes and she spoke out as with strong conviction, saying:

"I believe wholly—as wholly as I believe the Christian faith and that God has redeemed us from the fires of hell, that God speaks to me by that Voice!"

Being questioned further concerning the Voice, she said she was not at liberty to tell all she knew.

"Do you think God would be displeased at your telling the whole truth?"

"The Voice has commanded me to tell the King certain things, and not you — and some very lately — even last night; things which I would he knew. He would be more easy at his dinner."

"Why doesn't the Voice speak to the King itself, as it did when you were with him? Would it not if you asked it?"

"I do not know if it be the wish of God." She was pensive a moment or two, busy with her thoughts and far away, no doubt; then she added a remark in which Beaupere, always watchful, always alert, detected a possible opening — a chance to set a trap. Do you think he jumped at it instantly, betraying the joy he had in his find, as a young hand at craft and artifice would do? No, oh, no, you could not tell that he had noticed the remark at all. He slid indifferently away from it at once, and began to ask idle questions about other things, so as to slip around and spring on it from behind, so to speak: tedious and empty questions as to whether the Voice had told her she would escape from this prison; and if it had furnished answers to be used by her in to-day's seance; if it was accompanied with a glory of light; if it had eyes, etc. That risky remark of Joan's was this:

"Without the Grace of God I could do nothing."

The court saw the priest's game, and watched his play with a cruel eagerness. Poor Joan was grown dreamy and absent; possibly she was tired. Her life was in imminent danger, and she did not suspect it. The time was ripe now, and Beaupere quietly and stealthily sprung his trap:

"Are you in a state of Grace?"

Ah, we had two or three honorable brave men in that pack of judges; and Jean Lefevre was one of them. He sprang to his feet and cried out:

"It is a terrible question! The accused is not obliged to answer it!"

Cauchon's face flushed black with anger to see this plank flung to the perishing child, and he shouted:

"Silence! and take your seat. The accused will answer the question!"

There was no hope, no way out of the dilemma; for whether she said yes or whether she said no, it would be all the same—a disastrous answer, for the Scriptures had said one *cannot know* this thing. Think what hard hearts they were to set this fatal snare for that ignorant young girl and be proud of such work and happy in it. It was a miserable moment for me while we waited; it seemed a year. All the house showed excitement; and mainly it was glad excitement. Joan looked out upon these hungering faces with innocent, untroubled eyes, and then humbly and gently she brought out that immortal answer which brushed the formidable snare away as it had been but a cobweb:

"*If I be not in a state of Grace, I pray God place me in it; if I be in it, I pray God keep me so.*"

Ah, you will never see an effect like that; no, not

while you live. For a space there was the silence of the grave. Men looked wondering into each other's faces, and some were awed and crossed themselves; and I heard Lefevre mutter:

"It was beyond the wisdom of man to devise that answer. *Whence* come this child's amazing inspirations?"

Beaupere presently took up his work again, but the humiliation of his defeat weighed upon him, and he made but a rambling and dreary business of it, he not being able to put any heart in it.

He asked Joan a thousand questions about her childhood and about the oak wood, and the fairies, and the children's games and romps under our dear *Arbre Fée de Bourlemont*, and this stirring up of old memories broke her voice and made her cry a little, but she bore up as well as she could, and answered everything.

Then the priest finished by touching again upon the matter of her apparel—a matter which was never to be lost sight of in this still-hunt for this innocent creature's life, but kept always hanging over her, a menace charged with mournful possibilities:

"Would you like a woman's dress?"

"Indeed yes, if I may go out from this prison—but here, no."

CHAPTER VIII.

THE court met next on Monday the 27th. Would you believe it? The Bishop ignored the contract limiting the examination to matters set down in the *proces verbal* and again commanded Joan to take the oath without reservations. She said:

"You should be content I have sworn enough."

She stood her ground, and Cauchon had to yield.

The examination was resumed, concerning Joan's Voices.

"You have said that you recognized them as being the voices of angels the third time that you heard them. What angels were they?"

"St. Catherine and St. Marguerite."

"How did you know that it was those two saints? How could you tell the one from the other?"

"I know it was they; and I know how to distinguish them."

"By what sign?"

"By their manner of saluting me. I have been these seven years under their direction, and I knew who they were because they told me."

"Whose was the first Voice that came to you when you were thirteen years old?"

"It was the Voice of St. Michael. I saw him before my eyes; and he was not alone, but attended by a cloud of angels."

"Did you see the archangel and the attendant angels in the body, or in the spirit?"

"I saw them with the eyes of my body, just as I see you; and when they went away I cried because they did not take me with them."

It made me see that awful shadow again that fell dazzling white upon her that day under *l' Arbre Fée de Bourlemont*, and it made me shiver again, though it was so long ago. It was really not very long gone by, but it seemed so, because so much had happened since.

"In what shape and form did St. Michael appear?"

"As to that, I have not received permission to speak."

"What did the archangel say to you that first time?"

"I cannot answer you to-day."

Meaning, I think, that she would have to get permission of her Voices first.

Presently, after some more questions as to the revelations which had been conveyed through her to the King, she complained of the unnecessity of all this, and said:

"I will say again, as I have said before many times in these sittings, that I answered all questions of this sort before the court at Poitiers, and I would that you would bring here the record of that court and read from that. Prithee, send for that book."

There was no answer. It was a subject that had to be got around and put aside. That book had wisely been gotten out of the way, for it contained things which would be very awkward here. Among them was a decision that Joan's mission was from God, whereas it was the intention of this inferior court to show that it was from the devil; also a decision permitting Joan to wear male attire, whereas it was the purpose of this court to make the male attire do hurtful work against her.

"How was it that you were moved to come into France—by your own desire?"

"Yes, and by command of God. But that it was His will I would not have come. I would sooner have had my body torn in sunder by horses than come, lacking that."

Beaupere shifted once more to the matter of the male attire, now, and proceeded to make a solemn talk about it. That tried Joan's patience; and presently she interrupted and said:

"It is a trifling thing and of no consequence. And I did not put it on by counsel of any man, but by command of God."

"Robert de Baudricourt did not order you to wear it?"

"No."

"Do you think you did well in taking the dress of a man?"

"I did well to do whatsoever thing God commanded me to do."

"But in this particular case do you think you did well in taking the dress of a man?"

"I have done nothing but by command of God."

Beaupere made various attempts to lead her into contradictions of herself; also to put her words and acts in disaccord with the Scriptures. But it was lost time. He did not succeed. He returned to her visions, the light which shone about them, her relations with the King, and so on.

"Was there an angel above the King's head the first time you saw him?"

"By the Blessed Mary!—"

She forced her impatience down, and finished her sentence with tranquillity: "If there was one I did not see it."

"Was there light?"

"There were more than three hundred soldiers there, and five hundred torches, without taking account of spiritual light."

"What made the King believe in the revelations which you brought him?"

"He had signs; also the counsel of the clergy."

"What revelations were made to the King?"

"You will not get that out of me this year."

Presently she added: "During three weeks I was questioned by the clergy at Chinon and Poitiers. The King had a sign before he would believe; and the clergy were of opinion that my acts were good and not evil."

The subject was dropped now for a while, and Beaupere took up the matter of the miraculous sword of Fierbois to see if he could not find a chance there to fix the crime of sorcery upon Joan.

"How did you know that there was an ancient sword buried in the ground under the rear of the altar of the church of St. Catherine of Fierbois?"

Joan had no concealments to make as to this:

"I knew the sword was there because my Voices told me so; and I sent to ask that it be given to me to carry in the wars. It seemed to me that it was not very deep in the ground. The clergy of the church caused it to be sought for and dug up; and they polished it, and the rust fell easily off from it."

"Were you wearing it when you were taken in battle at Compiègne?"

"No. But I wore it constantly until I left St. Denis after the attack upon Paris."

This sword, so mysteriously discovered and so long and so constantly victorious, was suspected of being under the protection of enchantment.

"Was that sword blest? What blessing had been invoked upon it?"

"None. I loved it because it was found in the church of St. Catherine, for I loved that church very dearly."

She loved it because it had been built in honor of one of her angels.

"Didn't you lay it upon the altar, to the end that it might be lucky?" (The altar of St. Denis.)

"No."

"Didn't you pray that it might be made lucky?"

"Truly it were no harm to wish that my harness might be fortunate."

"Then it was not that sword which you wore in the field of Compiègne? What sword did you wear there?"

"The sword of the Burgundian Franquet d'Arras, whom I took prisoner in the engagement at Lagny. I kept it because it was a good war-sword—good to lay on stout thumps and blows with."

She said that quite simply; and the contrast between her delicate little self and the grim soldier-words which she dropped with such easy familiarity from her lips made many spectators smile.

"What is become of the other sword? Where is it now?"

"Is that in the *proces verbal?*"

Beaupere did not answer.

"Which do you love best, your banner or your sword?"

Her eye lighted gladly at the mention of her banner, and she cried out:

"I love my banner best—oh, forty times more than the sword! Sometimes I carried it myself when I charged the enemy, to avoid killing anyone." Then she added, naïvely, and with again that curious contrast between her girlish little personality and her subject, "I have never killed anyone."

It made a great many smile; and no wonder, when you consider what a gentle and innocent little thing she looked. One could hardly believe she had ever even seen men slaughtered, she looked so little fitted for such things.

"In the final assault at Orleans did you tell your soldiers that the arrows shot by the enemy and the stones discharged from their catapults and cannon would not strike any one but you?"

"No. And the proof is, that more than a hundred of my men were struck. I told them to have no doubts and no fears; that they would raise the siege. I was wounded in the neck by an arrow in the assault upon the bastille that commanded the bridge, but St. Catherine comforted me and I was cured in fifteen days without having to quit the saddle and leave my work."

"Did you know that you were going to be wounded?"

"Yes; and I had told it to the King beforehand. I had it from my Voices."

"When you took Jargeau, why did you not put its commandant to ransom?"

"I offered him leave to go out unhurt from the place, with all his garrison; and if he would not I would take it by storm."

"And you did, I believe."

"Yes."

"Had your Voices counseled you to take it by storm?"

"As to that, I do not remember."

Thus closed a weary long sitting, without result. Every device that could be contrived to trap Joan into wrong thinking, wrong doing, or disloyalty to the Church, or sinfulness as a little child at home or later had been tried, and none of them had succeeded. She had come unscathed through the ordeal.

Was the court discouraged? No. Naturally it was very much surprised, very much astonished, to find its work baffling and difficult instead of simple and easy, but it had powerful allies in the shape of hunger, cold, fatigue, persecution, deception, and treachery; and opposed to this array nothing but a defenseless and ignorant girl who must some time or other surrender to bodily and mental exhaustion or get caught in one of the thousand traps set for her.

And had the court made no progress during these seemingly resultless sittings? Yes. It had been feeling its way, groping here, groping there, and had found one or two vague trails which might freshen by and by and lead to something. The male attire, for instance, and the visions and Voices. Of course no one doubted that she had seen supernatural beings and been spoken to and advised by them. And of course no one doubted that by supernatural help miracles had been done by Joan, such as choosing out the King in a crowd when she had never seen him before, and her discovery of the sword buried under the altar. It would have been foolish to doubt these things, for we all know that the air is full of devils and angels that are visible to traffickers in magic on the one hand and to the stainlessly holy on the other; but what many and perhaps most did doubt was, that Joan's visions, voices, and miracles came from God. It was hoped that in time they could be proven to have been of satanic origin. Therefore, as you see, the court's persistent fashion of coming back to that subject every little while and spooking around it and prying into it was not to pass the time—it had a strictly business end in view.

CHAPTER IX.

THE next sitting opened on Thursday the first of March. Fifty-eight judges present — the others resting.

As usual, Joan was required to take an oath without reservations. She showed no temper this time. She considered herself well buttressed by the *proces verbal* compromise which Cauchon was so anxious to repudiate and creep out of; so she merely refused, distinctly and decidedly; and added, in a spirit of fairness and candor:

"But as to matters set down in the *proces verbal*, I will freely tell the whole truth — yes, as freely and fully as if I were before the Pope."

Here was a chance! We had two or three Popes, then; only one of them could be the true Pope, of course. Everybody judiciously shirked the question of *which* was the true Pope and refrained from naming him, it being clearly dangerous to go into particulars in this matter. Here was an opportunity to trick an unadvised girl into bringing herself into peril, and the unfair judge lost no time in taking advantage of it. He asked, in a plausibly indolent and absent way:

"Which one do you consider to be the true Pope?"

The house took an attitude of deep attention, and so waited to hear the answer and see the prey walk into the trap. But when the answer came it covered the judge with confusion, and you could see many people covertly chuckling. For Joan asked in a voice and manner which almost deceived even me, so innocent it seemed:

"Are there two?"

One of the ablest priests in that body and one of the best swearers there, spoke right out so that half the house heard him, and said:

"By God, it was a master stroke!"

As soon as the judge was better of his embarrassment he came back to the charge, but was prudent and passed by Joan's question:

"Is it true that you received a letter from the Count of Armagnac asking you which of the three Popes he ought to obey?"

"Yes, and answered it."

Copies of both letters were produced and read. Joan said that hers had not been quite strictly copied. She said she had received the Count's letter when she was just mounting her horse; and added:

"So, in dictating a word or two of reply I said I would try to answer him from Paris or somewhere where I could be at rest."

She was asked again which Pope she had considered the right one.

"I was not able to instruct the Count of Armagnac as to which one he ought to obey;" then she added, with a frank fearlessness which sounded fresh and wholesome in that den of trimmers and shufflers, "but as for me, I hold that we are bound to obey our Lord the Pope who is at Rome."

The matter was dropped. Then they produced and read a copy of Joan's first effort at dictating — her proclamation summoning the English to retire from the siege of Orleans and vacate France — truly a great and fine production for an unpracticed girl of seventeen.

"Do you acknowledge as your own the document which has just been read?"

"Yes, except that there are errors in it — words which make me give myself too much importance." I saw what was coming; I was troubled and ashamed. "For instance, I did not say 'Deliver up to the Maid' (*rendez à la Pucelle*); I said 'Deliver up to the King' (*rendez au Roi*); and I did not call myself 'Commander-in-Chief' (*chef de guerre*). All those are words which my secretary substituted; or mayhap he misheard me or forgot what I said."

She did not look at me when she said it: she spared me that embarrassment. I hadn't misheard her at all, and hadn't forgotten. I changed her language purposely, for she *was* Commander-in-Chief and entitled to call herself so, and it was becoming and proper, too; and who was going to surrender anything to the King? — at that time a stick, a cipher? If any surrendering was done, it would be to the noble Maid of Vaucouleurs, already famed and formidable though she had not yet struck a blow.

Ah, there would have been a fine and disagreeable episode (for me) there, if that pitiless court had discovered that the very scribbler of that piece of dictation, secretary to Joan of Arc, was present—and not only present, but helping build the record; and not only that, but destined at a far distant day to testify against lies and perversions smuggled into it by Cauchon and deliver them over to eternal infamy!

"Do you acknowledge that you dictated this proclamation?"

"I do."

"Have you repented of it? Do you retract it?"

Ah, then she was indignant!

"No! Not even these chains"—and she shook them—"not even these chains can chill the hopes that I uttered there. And more!"—she rose, and stood a moment with a divine strange light kindling in her face, then her words burst forth as in a flood—"I warn you now that before seven years a disaster will smite the English, oh, many fold greater than the fall of Orleans! and—"

"Silence! Sit down!"

"—and then, soon after, they will lose all France!"

Now consider these things. The French armies no longer existed. The French cause was standing still, our King was standing still, there was no hint that by and by the Constable Richemont would come forward and take up the great work of Joan of Arc and finish it. In face of all this, Joan made that prophecy—made it with perfect confidence—*and it came true.*

For within five years Paris fell—1436—and our King marched into it flying the victor's flag. So the first part of the prophecy was then fulfilled—in fact, almost the entire prophecy; for, with Paris in our hands, the fulfillment of the rest of it was assured.

Twenty years later all France was ours excepting a single town—Calais.

Now that will remind you of an earlier prophecy of Joan's. At the time that she wanted to take Paris and could have done it with ease if our King had but consented, she said that that was the golden time; that, with Paris ours, all France would be ours in six months. But if this golden opportunity to recover France was wasted, said she, "*I give you twenty years to do it in.*"

She was right. After Paris fell, in 1436, the rest of the work had to be done city by city, castle by castle, and it took twenty years to finish it.

Yes, it was the first day of March, 1431, there in the court, that she stood in the view of everybody and uttered that strange and incredible prediction. Now and then, in this world, somebody's prophecy turns up correct, but when you come to look into it there is sure to be considerable room for suspicion that the prophecy was made after the fact. But here the matter is different. There in that court Joan's prophecy was set down in the official record at the hour and moment of its utterance, years before the fulfillment, and there you may read it to this day. Twenty-five years after Joan's death the record was produced in the great Court of the Rehabilitation and verified under oath by Manchon and me, and surviving judges of our court confirmed the exactness of the record in their testimony.

Joan's startling utterance on that now so celebrated first of March stirred up a great turmoil, and it was some time before it quieted down again. Naturally, everybody was troubled, for a prophecy is a grisly and awful thing, whether one thinks it ascends from hell or comes down from heaven. All that these people felt sure of was, that the inspiration back of it was genuine and puissant. They would have given their right hands to know the source of it.

At last the questions began again.

"How do you know that those things are going to happen?"

"I know it by revelation. And I know it as surely as I know that you sit here before me."

This sort of answer was not going to allay the spreading uneasiness. Therefore, after some further dallying the judge got the subject out of the way and took up one which he could enjoy more.

"What language do your Voices speak?"

"French."

"St. Marguerite, too?"

"Verily; why not? She is on our side, not on the English?"

Saints and angels who did not condescend to speak English! a grave affront. They could not be brought into court and punished for contempt, but the tribunal could take silent note of Joan's remark and remember it against her; which they did. It might be useful by and by.

"Do your saints and angels wear jewelry?—crowns, rings, earrings?"

To Joan, questions like this were profane frivolities and not worthy of serious notice; she answered indifferently. But the question brought to her mind another matter, and she turned upon Cauchon and said:

"I had two rings. They have been taken away from me during my captivity. You have one of them. It is the gift of my brother. Give it back to me. If not to me, then I pray that it be given to the Church."

The judges conceived the idea that maybe these rings were for the working of enchantments. Perhaps they could be made to do Joan a damage.

"Where is the other ring?"

"The Burgundians have it."

"Where did you get it?"

"My father and mother gave it to me."

"Describe it."

"It is plain and simple and has '*Jesus and Mary*' engraved upon it."

Everybody could see that that was not a valuable equipment to do devil's work with. So that trail was not worth following. Still, to make sure, one of the judges asked Joan if she had ever cured sick people by touching them with the ring. She said no.

"Now as concerning the fairies, that were used to abide near by Domremy whereof there are many reports and traditions. It is said that your godmother surprised these creatures on a summer's night dancing under the tree called *l' Arbre Fée de Bourlemont.* Is it not possible that your pretended saints and angels are but those fairies?"

"Is that in your *proces ?*"

She made no other answer.

"Have you not conversed with St. Marguerite and St. Catherine under that tree?"

"I do not know."

"Or by the fountain near the tree?"

"Yes, sometimes."

"What promises did they make you?"

"None but such as they had God's warrant for."

"But what promises *did* they make?"

"That is not in your *proces ;* yet I will say this much: they told me that the King would become master of his kingdom in spite of his enemies."

"And what else?"

There was a pause; then she said humbly:

"They promised to lead me to Paradise."

If faces do really betray what is passing in men's minds, a fear came upon many in that house, at this time, that maybe, after all, a chosen servant and herald of God was here being hunted to her death. The interest deepened. Movements and whisperings ceased: the stillness became almost painful.

Have you noticed that almost from the beginning the nature of the questions asked Joan showed that in some way or other the questioner very often already knew his fact before he asked his question? Have you noticed that somehow or other the questioners usually knew just how and where to search for Joan's secrets; that they really knew the bulk of her privacies—a fact not suspected by her—and that they had no task before them but to trick her into exposing those secrets?

Do you remember Loyseleur, the hypocrite, the treacherous priest, tool of Cauchon? Do you remember that under the sacred seal of the confessional Joan freely and trustingly revealed to him everything concerning her history save only a few things regarding her supernatural revelations which her Voices had forbidden her to tell to anyone—and that the unjust judge, Cauchon, was a hidden listener all the time?

Now you understand how the inquisitors were able to devise that long array of minutely prying questions; questions whose subtlety and ingenuity and penetration are astonishing until we come to remember Loyseleur's performance and recognize their source. Ah, Bishop of Beauvais, you are now lamenting this cruel iniquity these many years in hell! Yes verily, unless one has come to your help. There is but one among the redeemed that would do it; and it is futile to hope that that one has not already done it—Joan of Arc.

We will return to the court and the questionings.

"Did they make you still another promise?"

"Yes, but that is not in your *proces*. I will not tell it now, but before three months I will tell it you."

The judge seems to know the matter he is asking about, already; one gets this idea from his next question.

"Did your Voices tell you that you would be liberated before three months?"

Joan often showed a little flash of surprise at the good guessing of the judges, and she showed one this time. I was frequently in terror to find my mind (which *I* could not control) criticising the Voices and saying, "They counsel her to speak boldly—a thing which she would do without any suggestion from *them* or anybody else—but when it comes to telling her any useful thing, such as how these conspirators manage to guess their way so skillfully into her affairs, they are always off attending to some other business."

I am reverent by nature; and when such thoughts swept through my head they made me cold with fear, and if there was a storm and thunder at the time, I was so ill that I could but with difficulty abide at my post and do my work.

Joan answered:

"That is not in your *proces*. I do not know when I shall be set free, but some who wish me out of this world will go from it before me."

It made some of them shiver.

"Have your Voices told you that you will be delivered from this prison?"

Without a doubt they had, and the judge knew it before he asked the question.

"Ask me again in three months and I will tell you." She said it with such a happy look, the tired prisoner! And I? And Noël Rainguesson, drooping yonder?—why, the floods of joy went streaming through us from crown to sole! It was all that we could do to hold still and keep from making fatal exposure of our feelings.

She was to be set free in three months. That was what she meant; we saw it. The Voices had told her so, and told her true—true to the very day—May 30th. But we know now that they had mercifully hidden from her *how* she was to be set free, but left her in ignorance. Home again! That was our understanding of it—Noël's and mine; that was our dream; and now we would count the days, the hours, the minutes. They would fly lightly along; they would soon be over. Yes, we would carry our idol home; and there, far from the pomps and tumults of the world, we would take up our happy life again and live it out as we had begun it, in the free air and the sunshine, with the friendly sheep and the friendly people for comrades, and the grace and charm of the meadows, the woods, and the river always before our eyes and their deep peace in our hearts. Yes, that was our dream, the dream that carried us bravely through that three months to an exact and awful fulfillment, the thought of which would have killed us, I think, if we had foreknown it and been obliged to bear the burden of it upon our hearts the half of those heavy days.

Our reading of the prophecy was this: We believed the King's soul was going to be smitten with remorse; and that he would privately plan a rescue with Joan's old lieutenants, D'Alençon and the Bastard and La Hire, and that this rescue would take place at the end of the three months. So we made up our minds to be ready and take a hand in it.

In the present and also in later sittings Joan was urged to name the exact day of her deliverance; but she could not do that. She had not the permission of her Voices. Moreover, the Voices themselves did not name the precise day. Ever since the fulfillment of the prophecy, I have believed that Joan had the idea that her deliverance was going to come in the form of death. But not *that* death! Divine as she was, dauntless as she was in battle, she was human also. She was not solely a saint, an angel, she was a claymade girl also — as human a girl as any in the world, and full of a human girl's sensitivenesses and tendernesses and delicacies. And so, *that* death! No, she could not have lived the three months with that one before her, I think. You remember that the first time she was wounded she was frightened, and cried, just as any other girl of seventeen would have done, although she had known for eighteen days that she was going to be wounded on that very day. No, she was not afraid of any ordinary death, and an ordinary death was what she believed the prophecy of deliverance meant, I think, for her face showed happiness, not horror, when she uttered it.

Now I will explain why I think as I do. Five weeks before she was captured in the battle of Compiègne, her Voices told her what was coming. They did not tell her the day or the place, but said she would be taken prisoner and that it would be before the feast of St. John. She begged that death, certain and swift, should be her fate, and the captivity brief; for she was a free spirit, and dreaded the confinement. The Voices made no promise, but only told her to bear whatever came. Now as they did not *refuse* the swift death, a hopeful young thing like Joan would naturally cherish that fact and make the most of it, allowing it to grow and establish itself in her mind. And so now that she was told she was to be "delivered" in three months, I think she believed it meant that she would die in her bed in the prison, and that that was why she looked happy and content—the gates of Paradise standing open for her, the time so short, you see, her troubles so soon to be over, her reward so close at hand. Yes, that would make her look happy, that would make her patient and bold, and able to fight her fight out like a soldier. Save herself if she could, of course, and try her best, for that was the way she was made; but die with her face to the front if die she must.

Then later, when she charged Cauchon with trying to kill her with a poisoned fish, her notion that she was to be "delivered" by death in the prison—if she had it, and I believe she had—would naturally be greatly strengthened, you see.

But I am wandering from the trial. Joan was asked to definitely name the time that she would be delivered from prison.

"I have always said that I was not permitted to tell you everything. I am to be set free, and I desire to ask leave of my Voices to tell you the day. This is why I wish for delay."

"Do your Voices forbid you to tell the truth?"

"Is it that you wish to know matters concerning the King of France? I tell you again that he will regain his kingdom, and that I know it as well as I know that you sit here before me in this tribunal." She sighed and, after a little pause, added: "I should be dead but for this revelation, which comforts me always."

Some trivial questions were asked her about St. Michael's dress and appearance. She answered them with dignity, but one saw that they gave her pain. After a little she said:

"I have great joy in seeing him, for when I see him I have the feeling that I am not in mortal sin." She added, "Sometimes St. Marguerite and St. Catherine have allowed me to confess myself to them."

Here was a possible chance to set a successful snare for her innocence.

"When you confessed were you in mortal sin, do you think?"

But her reply did her no hurt. So the inquiry was shifted once more to the revelations made to the King—secrets which the court had tried again and again to force out of Joan, but without success.

"Now as to the sign given to the King—"

"I have already told you that I will tell you nothing about it."

"Do you know what the sign was?"

"As to that, you will not find out from me."

All this refers to Joan's secret interview with the King—held apart, though two or three others were present. It was known—through Loyseleur, of course—that this sign was a crown and was a pledge of the verity of Joan's mission. But that is all a mystery until this day—the nature of the crown, I mean—and will remain a mystery to the end of time. We can never know whether a real crown descended upon the King's head, or only a symbol, the mystic fabric of a vision.

"Did you see a crown upon the King's head when he received the revelation?"

"I cannot tell you as to that, without perjury."

"Did the King have that crown at Rheims?"

"I think the King put upon his head a crown which he found there; but a much richer one was brought him afterwards."

"Have you seen that one?"

"I cannot tell you, without perjury. But whether I have seen it or not, I have heard say that it was rich and magnificent."

They went on and pestered her to weariness about that mysterious crown, but they got nothing more out of her. The sitting closed. A long, hard day for all of us.

CHAPTER X.

THE court rested a day, then took up work again on Saturday the third of March.

This was one of our stormiest sessions. The whole court was out of patience; and with good reason. These three-score distinguished churchmen, illustrious tacticians, veteran legal gladiators, had left important posts where their supervision was needed, to journey hither from various regions and accomplish a most simple and easy matter — condemn and send to death a country lass of nineteen who could neither read nor write, knew nothing of the wiles and perplexities of legal procedure, could call not a single witness in her defense, was allowed no advocate or adviser, and must conduct her case by herself against a hostile judge and a packed jury. In two hours she would be hopelessly entangled, routed, defeated, convicted. Nothing could be more certain than this — so they thought. But it was a mistake. The two hours had strung out into days; what promised to be a skirmish had expanded into a siege; the thing which had looked so easy had proven to be surprisingly difficult; the light victim who was to have been puffed away like a feather remained planted like a rock; and on top of all this, if anybody had a right to laugh it was the country lass and not the court.

She was not doing that, for that was not her spirit; but others were doing it. The whole town was laughing in its sleeve, and the court knew it, and its dignity was deeply hurt. The members could not hide their annoyance.

And so, as I have said, the session was stormy. It was easy to see that these men had made up their minds to force words from Joan to-day which should shorten up her case and bring it to a prompt conclusion. It shows that after all their experience with her they did not know her yet. They went into the battle with energy. They did not leave the questioning to a particular member; no, everybody helped. They volleyed questions at Joan from all over the house, and sometimes so many were talking at once that she had to ask them to deliver their fire one at a time and not by platoons. The beginning was as usual:

"You are once more required to take the oath pure and simple."

"I will answer to what is in the *proces verbal.* When I do more, I will choose the occasion for myself."

That old ground was debated and fought over inch by inch with great bitterness and many threats. But Joan remained steadfast, and the questionings had to shift to other matters. Half an hour was spent over Joan's apparitions — their dress, hair, general appearance, and so on — in the hope of fishing something of a damaging sort out of the replies; but with no result.

Next, the male attire was reverted to, of course. After many well-worn questions had been re-asked, one or two new ones were put forward.

"Did not the King or the Queen sometimes ask you to quit the male dress?"

"That is not in your *proces*."

"Do you think you would have sinned if you had taken the dress of your sex?"

"I have done best to serve and obey my sovereign Lord and Master."

After a while the matter of Joan's Standard was taken up, in the hope of connecting magic and witchcraft with it.

"Did not your men copy your banner in their pennons?"

"The lancers of my guard did it. It was to distinguish them from the rest of the forces. It was their own idea."

"Were they often renewed?"

"Yes. When the lances were broken they were renewed."

The purpose of the questions unveils itself in the next one.

"Did you not say to your men that pennons made like your banner would be lucky?"

The soldier-spirit in Joan was offended at this puerility. She drew herself up, and said with dignity and fire: "What I said to them was, 'Ride these English down!' and I did it myself."

Whenever she flung out a scornful speech like that at these French menials in English livery it lashed them into a rage; and that is what happened this time. There were ten, twenty, sometimes even thirty of them on their feet at a time, storming at the prisoner minute after minute, but Joan was not disturbed.

By and by there was peace, and the inquiry was resumed.

It was now sought to turn against Joan the thousand loving honors which had been done her when she was raising France out of the dirt and shame of a century of slavery and castigation.

"Did you not cause paintings and images of yourself to be made?"

"No. At Arras I saw a painting of myself kneeling in armor before the King and delivering him a letter; but I caused no such things to be made."

"Were not masses and prayers said in your honor?"

"If it was done it was not by my command. But if any prayed for me I think it was no harm."

"Did the French people believe you were sent of God?"

"As to that, I know not; but whether they believed it or not, I was not the less sent of God."

"If they thought you were sent of God do you think it was well thought?"

"If they believed it, their trust was not abused."

"What impulse was it, think you, that moved the people to kiss your hands, your feet, and your vestments?"

"They were glad to see me, and so they did those things; and I could not have prevented them if I had had the heart. Those poor people came lovingly to me because I had not done them any hurt, but had done the best I could for them according to my strength."

See what modest little words she uses to describe that touching spectacle, her marches about France walled in on both sides by the adoring multitudes: "They were glad to see me." Glad? Why, they were transported with joy to see her. When they could not kiss her hands or her feet, they knelt in the mire and kissed the hoof-prints of her horse. They worshiped her; and that is what these priests were trying to prove. It was nothing to them that she was not to blame for what other people did. No, if she was worshiped, it was enough; she was guilty of mortal sin. Curious logic, one must say.

"Did you not stand sponsor for some children baptized at Rheims?"

"At Troyes I did, and at St. Denis; and I named the boys Charles, in honor of the King, and the girls I named Joan."

"Did not women touch their rings to those which you wore?"

"Yes, many did, but I did not know their reason for it."

"At Rheims was your Standard carried into the church? Did you stand at the altar with it in your hand at the Coronation?"

"Yes."

"In passing through the country did you confess yourself in the churches and receive the sacrament?"

"Yes."

"In the dress of a man?"

"Yes. But I do not remember that I was in armor."

It was almost a concession! almost a half-surrender of the permission granted her by the Church at Poitiers to dress as a man. The wily court shifted to another matter: to pursue this one at this time might call Joan's attention to her small mistake, and by her native cleverness she might recover her lost ground. The tempestuous session had worn her and drowsed her alertness.

"It is reported that you brought a dead child to life in the church at Lagny. Was that in answer to your prayers?"

"As to that, I have no knowledge. Other young girls were praying for the child, and I joined them and prayed also, doing no more than they."

"Continue."

"While we prayed it came to life, and cried. It

had been dead three days, and was as black as my doublet. It was straightway baptized, then it passed from life again and was buried in holy ground."

"Why did you jump from the tower of Beaurevoir by night and try to escape?"

"I would go to the succor of Compiègne."

It was insinuated that this was an attempt to commit the deep crime of suicide to avoid falling into the hands of the English.

"Did you not say that you would rather die than be delivered into the power of the English?"

Joan answered frankly; without perceiving the trap:

"Yes; my words were, that I would rather that my soul be returned unto God than that I should fall into the hands of the English."

It was now insinuated that when she came to, after jumping from the tower, she was angry and blasphemed the name of God; and that she did it again when she heard of the defection of the Commandant of Soissons. She was hurt and indignant at this, and said:

"It is not true. I have never cursed. It is not my custom to swear."

CHAPTER XI.

A HALT was called. It was time. Cauchon was losing ground in the fight, Joan was gaining it. There were signs that here and there in the court a judge was being softened toward Joan by her courage, her presence of mind, her fortitude, her constancy, her piety, her simplicity and candor, her manifest purity, the nobility of her character, her fine intelligence, and the good brave fight she was making, all friendless and alone, against unfair odds, and there was grave room for fear that this softening process would spread further and presently bring Cauchon's plans in danger.

Something must be done, and it was done. Cauchon was not distinguished for compassion, but he now gave proof that he had it in his character. He thought it pity to subject so many judges to the prostrating fatigues of this trial when it could be conducted plenty well enough by a handful of them. Oh, gentle Judge! But he did not remember to modify the fatigues for the little captive.

He would let all the judges but a handful go, but he would select the handful himself, and he did.

He chose tigers. If a lamb or two got in, it was by oversight, not intention; and he knew what to do with lambs when discovered.

He called a small council now, and during five days they sifted the huge bulk of answers thus far gathered from Joan. They winnowed it of all chaff, all useless matter — that is, all matter favorable to Joan; they saved up all matter which could be twisted to her hurt, and out of this they constructed a basis for a new trial which should have the semblance of a continuation of the old one. Another change. It was plain that the public trial had wrought damage: its proceedings had been discussed all over the town and had moved many to pity the abused prisoner. There should be no more of that. The sittings should be secret hereafter, and no spectators admitted. So Noël could come no more. I sent this news to him. I had not the heart to carry it myself. I would give the pain a chance to modify before I should see him in the evening.

On the 10th of March the secret trial began. A week had passed since I had seen Joan. Her appearance gave me a great shock. She looked tired and weak. She was listless and far away, and her answers showed that she was dazed and not able to keep perfect run of all that was done and said. Another court would not have taken advantage of her state, seeing that her life was at stake here, but would have adjourned and spared her. Did this one? No; it worried her for hours, and with a glad and eager ferocity, making all it could out of this great chance, the first one it had had.

She was tortured into confusing herself concerning the "sign" which had been given the King, and the next day this was continued hour after hour. As a result, she made partial revealments of particulars forbidden by her Voices; and seemed to me to state as facts things which were but allegories and visions mixed with facts.

The third day she was brighter, and looked less worn. She was almost her normal self again, and did her work well. Many attempts were made to beguile her into saying indiscreet things, but she saw the purpose in view and answered with tact and wisdom.

"Do you know if St. Catherine and St. Marguerite hate the English?"

"They love whom Our Lord loves, and hate whom He hates."

"Does God hate the English?"

"Of the love or the hatred of God toward the English I know nothing." Then she spoke up with the old martial ring in her voice and the old audacity in her words, and added, "But I know this—that God will send victory to the French, and that all the English will be flung out of France but the dead ones!"

"Was God on the side of the English when they were *prosperous* in France?"

"I do not know if God hates the French, but I think that he allowed them to be chastised for their sins."

It was a sufficiently naïve way to account for a chastisement which had now strung out for ninety-six years. But nobody found fault with it. There was nobody there who would not punish a sinner ninety-six years if he could, nor anybody there who would ever dream of such a thing as the Lord's being any shade less stringent than men.

"Have you ever embraced St. Marguarite and St. Catherine?"

"Yes, both of them."

The evil face of Cauchon betrayed satisfaction when she said that.

"When you hung garlands upon *L'Arbre Fée de Bourlemont*, did you do it in honor of your apparitions?"

"No."

Satisfaction again. No doubt Cauchon would take it for granted that she hung them there out of sinful love for the fairies.

"When the saints appeared to you did you bow, did you make reverence, did you kneel?"

"Yes; I did them the most honor and the most reverence that I could."

A good point for Cauchon if he could eventually make it appear that these were no saints to whom she had done reverence, but devils in disguise.

Now there was the matter of Joan's keeping her

supernatural commerce a secret from her parents. Much might be made of that. In fact, particular emphasis had been given to it in a private remark written in the margin of the *proces* : "*She concealed her visions from her parents and from every one.*" Possibly this disloyalty to her parents might itself be the sign of the satanic source of her mission.

"Do you think it was right to go away to the wars without getting your parents' leave? It is written one must honor his father and his mother."

"I have obeyed them in all things but that. And for that I have begged their forgiveness in a letter and gotten it."

"Ah, you asked their pardon? So you *knew* you were guilty of sin in going without their leave!"

Joan was stirred. Her eyes flashed, and she exclaimed:

"I was commanded of God, and it was right to go! If I had had a hundred fathers and mothers and been a king's daughter to boot I would have gone."

"Did you never ask your Voices if you might tell your parents?"

"They were willing that I should tell them, but I would not for anything have given my parents that pain."

To the minds of the questioners this headstrong conduct savored of pride. That sort of pride would move one to seek sacrilegious adorations.

"Did not your Voices call you Daughter of God?"

Joan answered with simplicity, and unsuspiciously:

"Yes; before the siege of Orleans and since, they have several times called me Daughter of God."

Further indications of pride and vanity were sought.

"What horse were you riding when you were captured? Who gave it you?"

"The King."

"You had other things — riches — of the King?"

"For myself I had horses and arms, and money to pay the service in my household."

"Had you not a treasury?"

"Yes. Ten or twelve thousand crowns." Then she said with naïveté, "It was not a great sum to carry on a war with."

"You have it yet?"

"No. It is the King's money. My brothers hold it for him."

"What were the arms which you left as an offering in the church of St. Denis?"

"My suit of silver mail and a sword."

"Did you put them there in order that they might be adored?"

"No. It was but an act of devotion. And it is the custom of men of war who have been wounded to make such offering there. I had been wounded before Paris."

Nothing appealed to those stony hearts, those dull

imaginations — not even this pretty picture, so simply drawn, of the wounded girl-soldier hanging her toy harness there in curious companionship with the grim and dusty iron mail of the historic defenders of France. No, there was nothing in it for them; nothing, unless evil and injury for that innocent creature could be gotten out of it somehow.

"Which aided most — you the Standard, or the Standard you?"

"Whether it was the Standard or whether it was I, is nothing — the victories came from God."

"But did you base your hopes of victory in yourself or in your Standard?"

"In neither. In God, and not otherwhere."

"Was not your Standard waved around the King's head at the Coronation?"

"No. It was not."

"Why was it that *your* Standard had place at the crowning of the King in the Cathedral of Rheims, rather than those of the other captains?"

Then, soft and low, came that touching speech which will live as long as language lives, and pass into all tongues, and move all gentle hearts wheresoever it shall come, down to the latest day:

"*It had borne the burden, it had earned the honor.*"*

---

* What she said has been many times translated, but never with success. There is a haunting pathos about the original which eludes all efforts to convey it into our tongue. It is as subtle as an odor, and escapes in the transmission. Her words were these:

"*Il avait été a la peine, c'était bien raison qu'il fut a l' honneur.*"

How simple it is, and how beautiful. And how it beggars the studied eloquence of the masters of oratory. Eloquence was a native gift of Joan of Arc; it came from her lips without effort and without preparation. Her words were as sublime as her deeds, as sublime as her character; they had their source in a great heart and were coined in a great brain.

Monseigneur Ricard, Honorary Vicar-General to the Archbishop of Aix, finely speaks of it ("*Jeanne d' Arc la Vénérable*," page 197) as "that sublime reply, enduring in the history of celebrated sayings like the cry of a French and Christian soul wounded unto death in its patriotism and its faith."—TRANSLATOR.

CHAPTER XII.

NOW, as a next move, this small secret court of holy assassins did a thing so base that even at this day, in my old age, it is hard to speak of it with patience.

In the beginning of her commerce with her Voices there at Domremy, the child Joan solemnly devoted her life to God, vowing her pure body and her pure soul to his service. You will remember that her parents tried to stop her from going to the wars by haling her to the court at Toul to compel her to make a marriage which she had never promised to make — a marriage with our poor, good, windy, big, hard-fighting and most dear and lamented comrade, the Standard-Bearer, who fell in honorable battle and sleeps in God these sixty years, peace to his ashes! And you will remember how Joan, sixteen years old, stood up in that venerable court and conducted her case all by herself, and tore the poor Paladin's case to rags and blew it away with a breath; and how the astonished old judge on the bench spoke of her as "this marvelous child."

You remember all that. Then think what I felt, to see these false priests, here in the tribunal wherein

Joan had fought a fourth lone fight in three years, deliberately twist that matter entirely around and try to make out that Joan haled the Paladin into court and pretended that he had promised to marry her, and was bent on making him do it.

Certainly there was no baseness that those people were ashamed to stoop to in their hunt for that friendless girl's life. What they wanted to show was this — that she had committed the sin of relapsing from her vow and trying to violate it.

Joan detailed the true history of the case, but lost her temper as she went along, and finished with some words for Cauchon which he remembers yet, whether he is fanning himself in the world he belongs in or has swindled his way into the other.

The rest of this day and part of the next the court labored upon the old theme — the male attire. It was shabby work for those grave men to be engaged in; for they well knew one of Joan's reasons for clinging to the male dress was, that soldiers of the guard were always present in her room whether she was asleep or awake, and that the male dress was a better protection for her modesty than the other.

The court knew that one of Joan's purposes had been the deliverance of the exiled Duke of Orleans, and they were curious to know how she had intended to manage it. Her plan was characteristically business-like, and her statement of it as characteristically simple and straightforward:

"I would have taken English prisoners enough in France for his ransom; and failing that, I would have invaded England and brought him out by force."

That was just her way. If a thing was to be done, it was love first, and hammer and tongs to follow; but no shilly-shallying between. She added with a little sigh:

"If I had had my freedom three years, I would have delivered him."

"Have you the permission of your Voices to break out of prison whenever you can?"

"I have asked their leave several times, but they have not given it."

I think it is as I have said, she expected the deliverance of death, and within the prison walls, before the three months should expire.

"Would you escape if you saw the doors open?"

She spoke up frankly and said:

"Yes—for I should see in that the permission of Our Lord. God helps who help themselves, the proverb says. But except I thought I had permission, I would not go."

Now, then, at this point, something occurred which convinces me, every time I think of it—and it struck me so at the time—that for a moment, at least, her hopes wandered to the King, and put into her mind the same notion about her deliverance which Noël and I had settled upon—a rescue by her old soldiers. I think the idea of the rescue did occur to her, but only as a passing thought, and that it quickly passed away.

Some remark of the Bishop of Beauvais moved her to remind him once more that he was an unfair judge, and had no right to preside there, and that he was putting himself in great danger.

"What danger?" he asked.

"I do not know. St. Catherine has promised me help, but I do not know the form of it. I do not know whether I am to be delivered from this prison or whether when you send me to the scaffold there will happen a trouble by which I shall be set free. Without much thought as to this matter, I am of the opinion that it may be one or the other." After a pause she added these words, memorable forever — words whose meaning she may have mis-caught, misunderstood, as to that we can never know; words which she may have rightly understood; as to that also, we can never know; but words whose mystery fell away from them many a year ago and revealed their real meaning to all the world:

"But what my Voices have said clearest is, that I shall be delivered *by a great victory*." She paused, my heart was beating fast, for to me that great victory meant the sudden bursting in of our old soldiers with war-cry and clash of steel at the last moment and the carrying off of Joan of Arc in triumph. But, oh, that thought had such a short life! For now she raised her head and finished, with those solemn words which men still so often quote and dwell upon — words which filled me with fear, they sounded so like a prediction. "And always they say 'Submit to whatever comes; *do not grieve for your martyrdom;* from it you will ascend into the Kingdom of Paradise.'"

Was she thinking of fire and the stake? I think not. I thought of it myself, but I believe she was only thinking of this slow and cruel martyrdom of chains and captivity and insult. Surely, martyrdom was the right name for it.

It was Jean de la Fontaine who was asking the questions. He was willing to make the most he could out of what she had said:

"As the Voices have told you you are going to Paradise, you feel certain that that will happen and that you will not be damned in hell. Is that so?"

"I believe what they told me. I know that I shall be saved."

"It is a weighty answer."

"To me the knowledge that I shall be saved is a great treasure."

"Do you think that after that revelation you could be able to commit mortal sin?"

"As to that, I do not know. My hope for salvation is in holding fast to my oath to keep my body and my soul pure."

"Since you know you are to be saved do you think it necessary to go to confession?"

The snare was ingeniously devised, but Joan's simple and humble answer left it empty:

"One cannot keep his conscience too clean."

We were now arriving at the last day of this new trial. Joan had come through the ordeal well. It had been a long and wearisome struggle for all concerned. All ways had been tried to convict the accused, and all had failed, thus far. The inquisitors were thoroughly vexed and dissatisfied. However, they resolved to make one more effort, put in one more day's work. This was done—March 17th. Early in the sitting a notable trap was set for Joan:

"Will you submit to the determination of the Church all your words and deeds, whether good or bad?"

That was well planned. Joan was in imminent peril now. If she should heedlessly say yes, it would put her mission *itself* upon trial, and one would know how to decide its source and character promptly. If she should say no, she would render herself chargeable with the crime of heresy.

But she was equal to the occasion. She drew a distinct line of separation between the Church's authority over her as a subject member, and the matter of her *mission*. She said she loved the Church and was ready to support the Christian faith with all her strength; but as to the works done under her mission, those must be judged by God alone, who had commanded them to be done.

The judge still insisted that she submit them to the decision of the Church. She said:

"I will submit them to Our Lord who sent me.

It would seem to me that He and His Church are one, and that there should be no difficulty about this matter." Then she turned upon the judge and said, "Why do you make a difficulty where there is no room for any?"

Then Jean de la Fontaine corrected her notion that there was but one Church. There were two — the Church Triumphant, which is God, the saints, the angels, and the redeemed, and has its seat in heaven; and the Church Militant, which is our Holy Father the Pope, Vicar of God, the prelates, the clergy and all good Christians and Catholics, the which Church has its seat in the earth, is governed by the Holy Spirit, and cannot err. "Will you not submit those matters to the Church Militant?"

"I am come to the King of France from the Church Triumphant on high by its commandant, and to that Church I will submit all those things which I have done. For the Church Militant I have no other answer now."

The court took note of this straitly worded refusal, and would hope to get profit out of it; but the matter was dropped for the present, and a long chase was then made over the old hunting-ground — the fairies, the visions, the male attire, and all that.

In the afternoon the satanic Bishop himself took the chair and presided over the closing scenes of the trial. Along toward the finish, this question was asked by one of the judges:

"You have said to my lord the Bishop that you

would answer him as you would answer before our Holy Father the Pope, and yet there are several questions which you continually refuse to answer. Would you not answer the Pope more fully than you have answered before my lord of Beauvais? Would you not feel obliged to answer the Pope, who is the Vicar of God, more fully?"

Now fell a thunder-clap out of a clear sky:

"*Take me to the Pope.* I will answer to everything that I ought to."

It made the Bishop's purple face fairly blanch with consternation. If Joan had only known, if she had only known! She had lodged a mine under this black conspiracy able to blow the Bishop's schemes to the four winds of heaven, and she didn't know it. She had made that speech by mere instinct, not suspecting what tremendous forces were hidden in it, and there was none to tell her what she had done. I knew, and Manchon knew; and if she had known how to read writing we could have hoped to get the knowledge to her somehow; but speech was the only way, and none was allowed to approach her near enough for that. So there she sat, once more Joan of Arc the Victorious, but all unconscious of it. She was miserably worn and tired, by the long day's struggle and by illness, or she must have noticed the effect of that speech and divined the reason of it.

She had made many master-strokes, but this was *the* master-stroke. It was *an appeal to Rome.* It was her clear right; and if she had persisted in it Cauchon's plot would have tumbled about his ears like a house of cards, and he would have gone from that place the worst beaten man of the century. He was daring, but he was not daring enough to stand up against that demand if Joan had urged it. But no, she was ignorant, poor thing, and did not know what a blow she had struck for life and liberty.

France was not the Church. Rome had no interest in the destruction of this messenger of God. Rome would have given her a fair trial, and that was all that her cause needed. From that trial she would have gone forth free, and honored, and blessed.

But it was not so fated. Cauchon at once diverted the questions to other matters and hurried the trial quickly to an end.

As Joan moved feebly away, dragging her chains, I felt stunned and dazed, and kept saying to myself, "Such a little while ago she said the saving word and could have gone free; and now, there she goes to her death; yes, it is to her death, I know it, I feel it. They will double the guards; they will never let any come near her now between this and her condemnation, lest she get a hint and speak that word again. This is the bitterest day that has come to me in all this miserable time."

CHAPTER XIII.

SO the second trial in the prison was over. Over, and no definite result. The character of it I have described to you. It was baser in one particular than the previous one; for this time the charges had not been communicated to Joan, therefore she had been obliged to fight in the dark. There was no opportunity to do any thinking beforehand; there was no foreseeing what traps might be set, and no way to prepare for them. Truly it was a shabby advantage to take of a girl situated as this one was. One day, during the course of it, an able lawyer of Normandy, Maître Lohier, happened to be in Rouen, and I will give you his opinion of that trial, so that you may see that I have been honest with you, and that my partisanship has not made me deceive you as to its unfair and illegal character. Cauchon showed Lohier the *proces* and asked his opinion about the trial. Now this was the opinion which he gave to Cauchon. He said that the whole thing was null and void; for these reasons: 1, because the trial was secret, and full freedom of speech and action on the part of those present not possible; 2, because the trial touched the honor of the King of France, yet he was not summoned to defend himself, nor any one appointed to represent him; 3, because the charges against the prisoner were not communicated to her; 4, because the accused, although young and simple, had been forced to defend her cause without help of counsel, notwithstanding she had so much at stake.

Did that please Bishop Cauchon? It did not. He burst out upon Lohier with the most savage cursings, and swore he would have him drowned. Lohier escaped from Rouen and got out of France with all speed, and so saved his life.

Well, as I have said, the second trial was over, without definite result. But Cauchon did not give up. He could trump up another. And still another and another, if necessary. He had the half-promise of an enormous prize—the Archbishopric of Rouen—if he should succeed in burning the body and damning to hell the soul of this young girl who had never done him any harm; and such a prize as that, to a man like the Bishop of Beauvais, was worth the burning and damning of fifty harmless girls, let alone one.

So he set to work again straight off next day; and with high confidence, too, intimating with brutal cheerfulness that he should succeed this time. It took him and the other scavengers nine days to dig matter enough out of Joan's testimony and their own inventions to build up the new mass of charges.

And it was a formidable mass indeed, for it numbered sixty-six articles.

This huge document was carried to the castle the next day, March 27th; and there, before a dozen carefully-selected judges, the new trial was begun.

Opinions were taken, and the tribunal decided that Joan should hear the articles read this time. Maybe that was on account of Lohier's remark upon that head; or maybe it was hoped that the reading would kill the prisoner with fatigue — for, as it turned out, this reading occupied several days. It was also decided that Joan should bé required to answer squarely to every article, and that if she refused she should be considered *convicted*. You see, Cauchon was managing to narrow her chances more and more all the time; he was drawing the toils closer and closer.

Joan was brought in, and the Bishop of Beauvais opened with a speech to her which ought to have made even himself blush, so laden it was with hypocrisy and lies. He said that this court was composed of holy and pious churchmen whose hearts were full of benevolence and compassion toward her, and that they had no wish to hurt her body, but only a desire to instruct her and lead her into the way of truth and salvation.

Why, this man was born a devil; now think of his describing himself and those hardened slaves of his in such language as that.

And yet, worse was to come. For now having

in mind another of Lohier's hints, he had the cold effrontery to make to Joan a proposition which, I think, will surprise you when you hear it. He said that this court, recognizing her untaught estate and her inability to deal with the complex and difficult matters which were about to be considered, had determined, out of their pity and their mercifulness, to allow her to choose one or more persons *out of their own number* to help her with counsel and advice!

Think of that—a court made up of Loyseleur and his breed of reptiles. It was granting leave to a lamb to ask help of a wolf. Joan looked up to see if he was serious, and perceiving that he was at least pretending to be, she declined, of course.

The Bishop was not expecting any other reply. He had made a show of fairness and could have it entered on the minutes, therefore he was satisfied.

Then he commanded Joan to answer straitly to every accusation; and threatened to cut her off from the Church if she failed to do that or delayed her answers beyond a given length of time. Yes, he was narrowing her chances down, step by step.

Thomas de Courcelles began the reading of that interminable document, article by article. Joan answered to each article in its turn; sometimes merely denying its truth, sometimes by saying her answer would be found in the records of the previous trials.

What a strange document that was, and what an exhibition and exposure of the heart of man, the one creature authorized to boast that he is made in the image of God. To know Joan of Arc was to know one who was wholly noble, pure, truthful, brave, compassionate, generous, pious, unselfish, modest, blameless as the very flowers in the fields — a nature fine and beautiful, a character supremely great. To know her from that document would be to know her as the exact reverse of all that. Nothing that she *was* appears in it, everything that she was *not* appears there in detail.

Consider some of the things it charges against her, and remember who it is it is speaking of. It calls her a sorceress, a false prophet, an invoker and companion of evil spirits, a dealer in magic, a person ignorant of the Catholic faith, a schismatic; she is sacrilegious, an idolater, an apostate, a blasphemer of God and his saints, scandalous, seditious, a disturber of the peace; she incites men to war, and to the spilling of human blood; she discards the decencies and proprieties of her sex, irreverently assuming the dress of a man and the vocation of a soldier; she beguiles both princes and people; she usurps divine honors, and has caused herself to be adored and venerated, offering her hands and her vestments to be kissed.

There it is — every fact of her life distorted, perverted, reversed. As a child she had loved the fairies, she had spoken a pitying word for them when they were banished from their home, she had played under their tree and around their fountain —

hence she was a comrade of evil spirits. She had lifted France out of the mud and moved her to strike for freedom, and led her to victory after victory—hence she was a disturber of the peace—as indeed she was, and a provoker of war—as indeed she was again! and France will be proud of it and grateful for it for many a century to come. And she had been adored—as if she could help that, poor thing, or was in any way to blame for it. The cowed veteran and the wavering recruit had drunk the spirit of war from her eyes and touched her sword with theirs and moved forward invincible—hence she was a sorceress.

And so the document went on, detail by detail, turning these waters of life to poison, this gold to dross, these proofs of a noble and beautiful life to evidences of a foul and odious one.

Of course, the sixty-six articles were just a rehash of the things which had come up in the course of the previous trials, so I will touch upon this new trial but lightly. In fact, Joan went but little into detail herself, usually merely saying "That is not true—*passez outre;*" or, "I have answered that before—let the clerk read it in his record," or saying some other brief thing.

She refused to have her mission examined and tried by the earthly Church. The refusal was taken note of.

She denied the accusation of idolatry and that she had sought men's homage. She said:

"If any kissed my hands and my vestments it was not by my desire, and I did what I could to prevent it."

She had the pluck to say to that deadly tribunal that she did not know the fairies to be evil beings. She knew it was a perilous thing to say, but it was not in her nature to speak anything but the truth when she spoke at all. Danger had no weight with her in such things. Note was taken of her remark.

She refused, as always before, when asked if she would put off the male attire if she were given permission to commune. And she added this:

"When one receives the sacrament, the manner of his dress is a small thing and of no value in the eyes of Our Lord."

She was charged with being so stubborn in clinging to her male dress that she would not lay it off even to get the blessed privilege of hearing mass. She spoke out with spirit and said:

"I would rather die than be untrue to my oath to God."

She was reproached with doing man's work in the wars and thus deserting the industries proper to her sex. She answered, with some little touch of soldierly disdain:

"As to the matter of women's work, there's plenty to do it."

It was always a comfort to me to see the soldier-spirit crop up in her. While that remained in her she would be Joan of Arc, and able to look trouble and fate in the face.

"It appears that this mission of yours which you claim you had from God, was to make war and pour out human blood."

Joan replied quite simply, contenting herself with explaining that war was not her first move, but her second:

"To begin with, I demanded that peace should be made. If it was refused, then I would fight."

The judge mixed the Burgundians and English together in speaking of the enemy which Joan had come to make war upon. But she showed that she made a distinction between them by act and word, the Burgundians being Frenchmen and therefore entitled to less brusque treatment than the English. She said:

"As to the Duke of Burgundy, I required of him, both by letters and by his ambassadors, that he make peace with the King. As to the English, the only peace for them was that they leave the country and go home."

Then she said that even with the English she had shown a pacific disposition, since she had warned them away by proclamation before attacking them.

"If they had listened to me," said she, "they would have done wisely." At this point she uttered her prophecy again, saying with emphasis, "Before seven years they will see it themselves."

Then they presently began to pester her again

about her male costume, and tried to persuade her to voluntarily promise to discard it. I was never deep, so I think it no wonder that I was puzzled by their persistency in what seemed a thing of no consequence, and could not make out what their reason could be. But we all know now. We all know now that it was another of their treacherous projects. Yes, if they could but succeed in getting her to formally discard it they could play a game upon her which would quickly destroy her. So they kept at their evil work until at last she broke out and said:

"Peace! Without the permission of God I will not lay it off though you cut off my head!"

At one point she corrected the *proces verbal*, saying:

"It makes me say that everything which I have done was done by the counsel of Our Lord. I did not say that. I said 'all which I have *well* done.'"

Doubt was cast upon the authenticity of her mission because of the ignorance and simplicity of the messenger chosen. Joan smiled at that. She could have reminded these people that Our Lord, who is no respecter of persons, had chosen the lowly for his high purposes even oftener than he had chosen bishops and cardinals; but she phrased her rebuke in simpler terms:

"It is the prerogative of Our Lord to choose His instruments where He will."

She was asked what form of prayer she used in

invoking counsel from on high. She said the form was brief and simple; then she lifted her pallid face and repeated it, clasping her chained hands:

"Most dear God, in honor of your holy passion I beseech you, if you love me, that you will reveal to me what I am to answer to these churchmen. As concerns my dress, I know by what command I have put it on, but I know not in what manner I am to lay it off. I pray you tell me what to do."

She was charged with having dared, against the precepts of God and His saints, to assume empire over men and make herself Commander-in-Chief. That touched the soldier in her. She had a deep reverence for priests, but the soldier in her had but small reverence for a priest's opinions about war; so, in her answer to this charge she did not condescend to go into any explanations or excuses, but delivered herself with bland indifference and military brevity.

"If I was Commander-in-Chief, it was to thrash the English!"

Death was staring her in the face here all the time, but no matter; she dearly loved to make these English-hearted Frenchmen squirm, and whenever they gave her an opening she was prompt to jab her sting into it. She got great refreshment out of these little episodes. Her days were a desert; these were the oases in it.

Her being in the wars with men was charged against her as an indelicacy. She said:

"I had a woman with me when I could—in towns and lodgings. In the field I always slept in my armor."

That she and her family had been ennobled by the King was charged against her as evidence that the source of her deeds were sordid self-seeking. She answered that she had not asked this grace of the King, it was his own act.

This third trial was ended at last. And once again there was no definite result.

Possibly a fourth trial might succeed in defeating this apparently unconquerable girl. So the malignant Bishop set himself to work to plan it.

He appointed a commission to reduce the substance of the sixty-six articles to twelve compact lies, as a basis for the new attempt. This was done. It took several days.

Meantime Cauchon went to Joan's cell one day, with Manchon and two of the judges, Isambard de la Pierre and Martin Ladvenue, to see if he could not manage somehow to beguile Joan into submitting her mission to the examination and decision of the church militant—that is to say, to that part of the church militant which was represented by himself and his creatures.

Joan once more positively refused. Isambard de la Pierre had a heart in his body, and he so pitied this persecuted poor girl that he ventured to do a very daring thing; for he asked her if she would be willing to have her case go before the Council of

Basel, and said it contained as many priests of her party as of the English party.

Joan cried out that she would gladly go before so fairly constructed a tribunal as that; but before Isambard could say another word Cauchon turned savagely upon him and exclaimed:

"Shut up, in the devil's name!"

Then Manchon ventured to do a brave thing, too, though he did it in great fear for his life. He asked Cauchon if he should enter Joan's submission to the Council of Basel upon the minutes.

"No! It is not necessary."

"Ah," said poor Joan, reproachfully, "you set down everything that is against me, but you will not set down what is for me."

It was piteous. It would have touched the heart of a brute. But Cauchon was more than that.

CHAPTER XIV.

WE were now in the first days of April. Joan was ill. She had fallen ill the 29th of March, the day after the close of the third trial, and was growing worse when the scene which I have just described occurred in her cell. It was just like Cauchon to go there and try to get some advantage out of her weakened state.

Let us note some of the particulars in the new indictment — the Twelve Lies.

Part of the first one says Joan asserts that she has found her salvation. She never said anything of the kind. It also says she refuses to submit herself to the Church. Not true. She was willing to submit all her acts to this Rouen tribunal except those done by command of God in fulfillment of her mission. Those she reserved for the judgment of God. She refused to recognize Cauchon and his serfs as the Church, but was willing to go before the Pope or the Council of Basel.

A clause of another of the Twelve says she admits having threatened with death those who would not obey her. Distinctly false. Another clause says she declares that all she has done has been done by command of God. What she really said was, all that she had done *well*—a correction made by herself as you have already seen.

Another of the Twelve says she claims that she has never committed any sin. She never made any such claim.

Another makes the wearing of the male dress a sin. If it was, she had high Catholic authority for committing it—that of the Archbishop of Rheims and the tribunal of Poitiers.

The Tenth Article was resentful against her for "pretending" that St. Catherine and St. Marguerite spoke French and not English, and were French in their politics.

The Twelve were to be submitted first to the learned doctors of theology of the University of Paris for approval. They were copied out and ready by the night of April 4th. Then Manchon did another bold thing: he wrote in the margin that many of the Twelve put statements in Joan's mouth which were the exact opposite of what she had said. *That* fact would not be considered important by the University of Paris, and would not influence its decision or stir its humanity, in case it had any—which it hadn't when acting in a political capacity, as at present—but it was a brave thing for that good Manchon to do, all the same.

The Twelve were sent to Paris next day, April 5th. That afternoon there was a great tumult in

Rouen, and excited crowds were flocking through all the chief streets, chattering and seeking for news; for a report had gone abroad that Joan of Arc was sick unto death. In truth, these long seances had worn her out, and she was ill indeed. The heads of the English party were in a state of consternation; for if Joan should die uncondemned by the Church and go to the grave unsmirched, the pity and the love of the people would turn her wrongs and sufferings and death into a holy martyrdom, and she would be even a mightier power in France dead than she had been when alive.

The Earl of Warwick and the English Cardinal (Winchester) hurried to the castle and sent messengers flying for physicians. Warwick was a hard man, a rude, coarse man, a man without compassion. There lay the sick girl stretched in her chains in her iron cage — not an object to move man to ungentle speech, one would think; yet Warwick spoke right out in her hearing and said to the physicians:

"Mind you take good care of her. The King of England has no mind to have her die a natural death. She is dear to him, for he bought her dear, and he does not want her to die, save at the stake. Now then, mind you cure her."

The doctors asked Joan what had made her ill. She said the Bishop of Beauvais had sent her a fish and she thought it was that.

Then Jean d'Estivet burst out on her, and called her names and abused her. He understood Joan to be charging the Bishop with poisoning her, you see; and that was not pleasing to him, for he was one of Cauchon's most loving and conscienceless slaves, and it outraged him to have Joan injure his master in the eyes of these great English chiefs, these being men who could ruin Cauchon and would promptly do it if they got the conviction that he was capable of saving Joan from the stake by poisoning her and thus cheating the English out of all the real value gainable by her purchase from the Duke of Burgundy.

Joan had a high fever, and the doctors proposed to bleed her. Warwick said:

"Be careful about that; she is smart and is capable of killing herself."

He meant that to escape the stake she might undo the bandage and let herself bleed to death.

But the doctors bled her anyway, and then she was better.

Not for long, though. Jean d'Estivet could not hold still, he was so worried and angry about the suspicion of poisoning which Joan had hinted at; so he came back in the evening and stormed at her till he brought the fever all back again.

When Warwick heard of this he was in a fine temper, you may be sure, for here was his prey threatening to escape again, and all through the over-zeal of this meddling fool. Warwick gave D'Estivet a quite admirable cursing—admirable as to strength, I mean, for it was said by persons of culture that the art of it was not good — and after that the meddler kept still.

Joan remained ill more than two weeks; then she grew better. She was still very weak, but she could bear a little persecution now without much danger to her life. It seemed to Cauchon a good time to furnish it. So he called together some of his doctors of theology and went to her dungeon. Manchon and I went along to keep the record — that is, to set down what might be useful to Cauchon, and leave out the rest.

The sight of Joan gave me a shock. Why, she was but a shadow! It was difficult for me to realize that this frail little creature with the sad face and drooping form was the same Joan of Arc that I had so often seen, all fire and enthusiasm, charging through a hail of death and the lightning and thunder of the guns at the head of her battalions. It wrung my heart to see her looking like this.

But Cauchon was not touched. He made another of those conscienceless speeches of his, all dripping with hypocrisy and guile. He told Joan that among her answers had been some which had seemed to endanger religion; and as she was ignorant and without knowledge of the Scriptures, he had brought some good and wise men to instruct her, if she desired it. Said he, "We are churchmen, and disposed by our good will as well as by our vocation to procure for you the salvation of your soul and your body, in every way in our power, just as we would do the like for our nearest kin or for ourselves. In this we but follow the example of Holy Church, who never closes the refuge of her bosom against any that are willing to return."

Joan thanked him for these sayings and said:

"I seem to be in danger of death from this malady; if it be the pleasure of God that I die here, I beg that I may be heard in confession and also receive my Saviour; and that I may be buried in consecrated ground."

Cauchon thought he saw his opportunity at last; this weakened body had the fear of an unblessed death before it and the pains of hell to follow. This stubborn spirit would surrender now. So he spoke out and said:

"Then if you want the Sacraments, you must do as all good Catholics do, and submit to the Church."

He was eager for her answer; but when it came there was no surrender in it, she still stood to her guns. She turned her head away and said wearily:

"I have nothing more to say."

Cauchon's temper was stirred, and he raised his voice threateningly and said that the more she was in danger of death the more she ought to amend her life; and again he refused the things she begged for unless she would submit to the Church. Joan said:

"If I die in this prison I beg you to have me buried in holy ground; if you will not, I cast myself upon my Saviour."

There was some more conversation of the like sort,

then Cauchon demanded again, and imperiously, that she submit herself and all her deeds to the Church. His threatening and storming went for nothing. That body was weak, but the spirit in it was the spirit of Joan of Arc; and out of that came the steadfast answer which these people were already so familiar with and detested so sincerely:

"Let come what may, I will neither do nor say any otherwise than I have said already in your tribunals."

Then the good theologians took turn about and worried her with reasonings and arguments and Scriptures; and always they held the lure of the Sacraments before her famishing soul, and tried to bribe her with them to surrender her mission to the Church's judgment—that is to *their* judgment—as if *they* were the Church! But it availed nothing. I could have told them that beforehand, if they had asked me. But they never asked me anything; I was too humble a creature for their notice.

Then the interview closed with a threat; a threat of fearful import; a threat calculated to make a Catholic Christian feel as if the ground were sinking from under him:

"The Church calls upon you to submit; disobey, and she will abandon you as if you were a pagan!"

Think of being abandoned by the Church!—that august Power in whose hands is lodged the fate of the human race; whose scepter stretches beyond the furthest constellation that twinkles in the sky; whose authority is over the millions that live and over the billions that wait trembling in purgatory for ransom or doom; whose smile opens the gates of Heaven to you, whose frown delivers you to the fires of everlasting hell; a Power whose dominion overshadows and belittles earthly empire as earthly empire overshadows and belittles the pomps and shows of a village. To be abandoned by one's King — yes, that is death, and death is much; but to be abandoned by Rome, to be abandoned by the Church! Ah, death is nothing to that, for that is consignment to endless *life* — and such a life!

I could see the red waves tossing in that shoreless lake of fire, I could see the black myriads of the damned rise out of them and struggle and sink and rise again; and I knew that Joan was seeing what I saw, while she paused musing; and I believed that she must yield now, and in truth I hoped she would, for these men were able to make the threat good and deliver her over to eternal suffering, and I knew that it was in their natures to do it.

But I was foolish to think that thought and hope that hope. Joan of Arc was not made as others are made. Fidelity to principle, fidelity to truth, fidelity to her word, all these were in her bone and in her flesh — they were parts of her. She could not change, she could not cast them out. She was the very genius of Fidelity, she was Steadfastness incarnated. Where she had taken her stand and planted her foot, there she would abide; hell itself could not move her from that place.

Her Voices had not given her permission to make the sort of submission that was required, therefore she would stand fast. She would wait, in perfect obedience, let come what might.

My heart was like lead in my body when I went out from that dungeon; but she — she was serene, she was not troubled. She had done what she believed to be her duty, and that was sufficient; the consequences were not her affair. The last thing she said that time was full of this serenity, full of contented repose:

"I am a good Christian born and baptized, and a good Christian I will die."

CHAPTER XV.

TWO weeks went by; the second of May was come, the chill was departed out of the air, the wild flowers were springing in the glades and glens, the birds were piping in the woods, all nature was brilliant with sunshine, all spirits were renewed and refreshed, all hearts glad, the world was alive with hope and cheer, the plain beyond the Seine stretched away soft and rich and green, the river was limpid and lovely, the leafy islands were dainty to see, and flung still daintier reflections of themselves upon the shining water; and from the tall bluffs above the bridge Rouen was become again a delight to the eye, the most exquisite and satisfying picture of a town that nestles under the arch of heaven anywhere.

When I say that all hearts were glad and hopeful, I mean it in a general sense. There were exceptions —we who were the friends of Joan of Arc, also Joan of Arc herself, that poor girl shut up there in that frowning stretch of mighty walls and towers: brooding in darkness, so close to the flooding downpour of sunshine yet so impossibly far away from it;

so longing for any little glimpse of it, yet so implacably denied it by those wolves in the black gowns who were plotting her death and the blackening of her good name.

Cauchon was ready to go on with his miserable work. He had a new scheme to try now. He would see what persuasion could do — argument, eloquence, poured out upon the incorrigible captive from the mouth of a trained expert. That was his plan. But the reading of the Twelve Articles to her was not a part of it. No, even Cauchon was ashamed to lay that monstrosity before her; even he had a remnant of shame in him, away down deep, a million fathoms deep, and that remnant asserted itself now and prevailed.

On this fair second of May, then, the black company gathered itself together in the spacious chamber at the end of the great hall of the castle — the Bishop of Beauvais on his throne, and sixty-two minor judges massed before him, with the guards and recorders at their stations and the orator at his desk.

Then we heard the far clank of chains, and presently Joan entered with her keepers and took her seat upon her isolated bench. She was looking well now, and most fair and beautiful after her fortnight's rest from wordy persecution.

She glanced about and noted the orator. Doubtless she divined the situation.

The orator had written his speech all out, and had it in his hand, though he held it back of him out of sight. It was so thick that it resembled a book. He began flowingly, but in the midst of a flowery period his memory failed him and he had to snatch a furtive glance at his manuscript—which much injured the effect. Again this happened, and then a third time. The poor man's face was red with embarrassment, the whole great house was pitying him, which made the matter worse; then Joan dropped in a remark which completed his trouble. She said:

"*Read your book*—and then I will answer you!"

Why, it was almost cruel the way those mouldy veterans laughed; and as for the orator, he looked so flustered and helpless that almost anybody would have pitied him, and I had difficulty to keep from doing it myself. Yes, Joan was feeling very well after her rest, and the native mischief that was in her lay near the surface. It did not show when she made the remark, but I knew it was close in there back of the words.

When the orator had gotten back his composure he did a wise thing; for he followed Joan's advice: he made no more attempts at sham impromptu oratory, but read his speech straight from his "book." In the speech he compressed the Twelve Articles into six and made these his text.

Every now and then he stopped and asked questions, and Joan replied. The nature of the church militant was explained, and once more Joan was asked to submit herself to it.

She gave her usual answer.

Then she was asked:

"Do you believe the Church can err?"

"I believe it cannot err; but for those deeds and words of mine which were done and uttered by command of God, I will answer to Him alone."

"Will you say that you have no judge upon earth? Is not our Holy Father the Pope your judge?"

"I will say nothing to you about it. I have a good Master who is our Lord and to Him I will submit all."

Then came these terrible words:

"If you do not submit to the Church you will be pronounced a heretic by these judges here present and burned at the stake!"

Ah, that would have smitten you or me dead with fright, but it only roused the lion heart of Joan of Arc, and in her answer rang that martial note which had used to stir her soldiers like a bugle-call:

"I will not say otherwise than I have said already; and if I saw the fire before me I would say it again!"

It was uplifting to hear her battle-voice once more and see the battle-light burn in her eye. Many there were stirred; every man that was a *man* was stirred, whether friend or foe; and Manchon risked his life again, good soul, for he wrote in the margin of the record in good plain letters these brave words: "*Superba responsio!*" and there they have remained these sixty years, and there you may read them to this day.

"*Superba responsio!*" Yes, it was just that. For this "superb answer" came from the lips of a girl of nineteen with death and hell staring her in the face.

Of course, the matter of the male attire was gone over again; and as usual at wearisome length; also, as usual, the customary bribe was offered: if she would discard that dress voluntarily they would let her hear mass. But she answered as she had often answered before:

"I will go in a woman's robe to all services of the church if I may be permitted, but I will resume the other dress when I return to my cell."

They set several traps for her in a tentative form; that is to say, they placed supposititious propositions before her and cunningly tried to commit her to one end of the propositions without committing themselves to the other. But she always saw the game and spoiled it. The trap was in this form:

"Would you be willing to do so and so if we should give you leave?"

Her answer was always in this form or to this effect:

"When you give me leave, then you will know."

Yes, Joan was at her best that second of May. She had all her wits about her, and they could not catch her anywhere. It was a long, long session, and all the old ground was fought over again, foot by foot, and the orator-expert worked all his persuasions, all his eloquence; but the result was the familiar one — a drawn battle, the sixty-two retiring upon their base, the solitary enemy holding her original position within her original lines.

CHAPTER XVI.

THE brilliant weather, the heavenly weather, the bewitching weather made everybody's heart to sing, as I have told you; yes, Rouen was feeling light-hearted and gay, and most willing and ready to break out and laugh upon the least occasion; and so when the news went around that the young girl in the tower had scored another defeat against Bishop Cauchon there was abundant laughter—abundant laughter among the citizens of both parties, for they all hated the Bishop. It is true, the English-hearted majority of the people wanted Joan burned, but that did not keep them from laughing at the man they hated. It would have been perilous for anybody to laugh at the English chiefs or at the majority of Cauchon's assistant judges, but to laugh at Cauchon or D'Estivet and Loyseleur was safe—nobody would report it.

The difference between Cauchon and *cochon** was not noticeable in speech, and so there was plenty of opportunity for puns; the opportunities were not thrown away.

* Hog, pig.

Some of the jokes got well worn in the course of two or three months, from repeated use; for every time Cauchon started a new trial the folk said "The sow has littered* again"; and every time the trial failed they said it over again, with its other meaning, "The hog has made a mess of it."

And so, on the third of May, Noël and I, drifting about the town, heard many a wide-mouthed lout let go his joke and his laugh, and then move to the next group, proud of his wit and happy, to work it off again:

"'Ods blood, the sow has littered five times, and five times has made a mess of it!"

And now and then one was bold enough to say—but he said it softly:

"Sixty-three and the might of England against a girl, and she camps on the field five times!"

Cauchon lived in the great palace of the Archbishop, and it was guarded by English soldiery; but no matter, there was never a dark night but the walls showed next morning that the rude joker had been there with his paint and brush. Yes, he had been there, and had smeared the sacred walls with pictures of hogs in all attitudes except flattering ones; hogs clothed in a Bishop's vestments and wearing a Bishop's mitre irreverently cocked on the side of their heads.

Cauchon raged and cursed over his defeats and his impotence during seven days, then he conceived a

* *Cochonner*, to litter, to farrow; also, "to make a mess of!"

new scheme. You shall see what it was; for you have not cruel hearts, and you would never guess it.

On the ninth of May there was a summons, and Manchon and I got our materials together and started. But this time we were to go to one of the other towers — not the one which was Joan's prison. It was round and grim and massive, and built of the plainest and thickest and solidest masonry — a dismal and forbidding structure.*

We entered the circular room on the ground floor, and I saw what turned me sick — the instruments of torture and the executioners standing ready! Here you have the black heart of Cauchon at the blackest, here you have the proof that in his nature there was no such thing as pity. One wonders if he ever knew his mother or ever had a sister.

Cauchon was there, and the Vice-Inquisitor and the Abbot of St. Corneille; also six others, among them that false Loyseleur. The guards were in their places, the rack was there, and by it stood the executioner and his aids in their crimson hose and doublets, meet color for their bloody trade. The picture of Joan rose before me stretched upon the rack, her feet tied to one end of it, her wrists to the other, and those red giants turning the windlass and pulling her limbs out of their sockets. It seemed to me that I could hear the bones snap and the flesh tear apart, and I did not see how that body of

* The lower half of it remains to-day just as it was then; the upper half is of a later date.— TRANSLATOR.

anointed servants of the merciful Jesus could sit there and look so placid and indifferent.

After a little, Joan arrived and was brought in. She saw the rack, she saw the attendants, and the same picture which I had been seeing must have risen in her mind; but do you think she quailed, do you think she shuddered? No, there was no sign of that sort. She straightened herself up, and there was a slight curl of scorn about her lip; but as for fear, she showed not a vestige of it.

This was a memorable session, but it was the shortest one of all the list. When Joan had taken her seat a résumé of her "crimes" was read to her. Then Cauchon made a solemn speech. In it he said that in the course of her several trials Joan had refused to answer some of the questions and had answered others with lies, but that now he was going to have the truth out of her, and the whole of it.

His manner was full of confidence this time; he was sure he had found a way at last to break this child's stubborn spirit and make her beg and cry. He would score a victory this time and stop the mouths of the jokers of Rouen. You see, he was only just a man after all, and couldn't stand ridicule any better than other people. He talked high, and his splotchy face lighted itself up with all the shifting tints and signs of evil pleasure and promised triumph — purple, yellow, red, green — they were all there, with sometimes the dull and spongy blue of a drowned man, the uncanniest of them all. And finally he burst out in a great passion and said:

"There is the rack, and there are its ministers! You will reveal all now or be put to the torture. Speak."

Then she made that great answer which will live forever; made it without fuss or bravado, and yet how fine and noble was the sound of it:

"I will tell you nothing more than I have told you; no, not even if you tear the limbs from my body. And even if in my pain I *did* say something other wise, I would always say afterwards that it was the torture that spoke and not I."

There was no crushing that spirit. You should have seen Cauchon. Defeated again, and he had not dreamed of such a thing. I heard it said next day, around the town, that he had a full confession, all written out, in his pocket and all ready for Joan to sign. I do not know that that was true, but it probably was, for her mark signed at the bottom of a confession would be the kind of evidence (for effect with the public) which Cauchon and his people would particularly value, you know.

No, there was no crushing that spirit, and no beclouding that clear mind. Consider the depth, the wisdom of that answer, coming from an ignorant girl. Why, there were not six men in the world who had ever reflected that words forced out of a person by horrible tortures were not necessarily words of verity and truth, yet this unlettered peasant girl put her finger upon that flaw with an unerring instinct. I had always supposed that torture brought out the truth — everybody supposed it; and when Joan came out with those simple common-sense words they seemed to flood the place with light. It was like a lightning-flash at midnight which suddenly reveals a fair valley sprinkled over with silver streams and gleaming villages and farmsteads where was only an impenetrable world of darkness before. Manchon stole a sidewise look at me, and his face was full of surprise; and there was the like to be seen in other faces there. Consider — they were old, and deeply cultured, yet here was a village maid able to teach them something which they had not known before. I heard one of them mutter:

"Verily it is a wonderful creature. She has laid her hand upon an accepted truth that is as old as the world, and it has crumbled to dust and rubbish under her touch. Now whence got she that marvelous insight?"

The judges laid their heads together and began to talk low. It was plain, from chance words which one caught now and then, that Cauchon and Loyseleur were insisting upon the application of the torture, and that most of the others were urgently objecting.

Finally Cauchon broke out with a good deal of asperity in his voice and ordered Joan back to her dungeon. That was a happy surprise for me. I was not expecting that the Bishop would yield.

When Manchon came home that night he said he had found out why the torture was not applied. There were two reasons. One was, a fear that Joan might die under the torture, which would not suit the English at all; the other was, that the torture would effect nothing if Joan was going to take back everything she said under its pains; and as to putting her mark to a confession, it was believed that not even the rack could ever make her do that.

So all Rouen laughed again, and kept it up for three days, saying:

"The sow has littered six times, and made six messes of it."

And the palace walls got a new decoration — a mitred hog carrying a discarded rack home on its shoulder, and Loyseleur weeping in its wake. Many rewards were offered for the capture of these painters, but nobody applied. Even the English guard feigned blindness and would not see the artists at work.

The Bishop's anger was very high now. He could not reconcile himself to the idea of giving up the torture. It was the pleasantest idea he had invented yet, and he would not cast it by. So he called in some of his satellites on the twelfth, and urged the torture again. But it was a failure. With some, Joan's speech had wrought an effect; others feared she might die under the torture; others did not believe that any amount of suffering could make her put her mark to a lying confession. There were fourteen men present, including the Bishop. Eleven of them voted dead against the torture, and stood their ground in spite of Cauchon's abuse. Two voted with the Bishop and insisted upon the torture. These two were Loyseleur and the orator — the man whom Joan had bidden to "read his book" — Thomas de Courcelles, the renowned pleader, and master of eloquence.

Age has taught me charity of speech; but it fails me when I think of those three names — Cauchon, Courcelles, Loyseleur.

CHAPTER XVII.

ANOTHER ten days' wait. The great theologians of that treasury of all valuable knowledge and all wisdom, the University of Paris, were still weighing and considering and discussing the Twelve Lies.

I had but little to do these ten days, so I spent them mainly in walks about the town with Noël. But there was no pleasure in them, our spirits being so burdened with cares, and the outlook for Joan growing so steadily darker and darker all the time. And then we naturally contrasted our circumstances with hers: this freedom and sunshine, with her darkness and chains; our comradeship, with her lonely estate; our alleviations of one sort and another, with her destitution in all. She was used to liberty, but now she had none; she was an out-of-door creature by nature and habit, but now she was shut up day and night in a steel cage like an animal; she was used to the light, but now she was always in a gloom where all objects about her were dim and spectral; she was used to the thousand various sounds which are the cheer and music of a busy life, but now she heard only the monotonous footfall of the sentry pacing his watch; she had been fond of talking with her mates, but now there was no one to talk to; she had had an easy laugh, but it was gone dumb now; she had been born for comradeship, and blithe and busy work, and all manner of joyous activities, but here were only dreariness, and leaden hours, and weary inaction, and brooding stillness, and thoughts that travel day and night and night and day round and round in the same circle, and wear the brain and break the heart with weariness. It was death in life; yes, death in life, that is what it must have been. And there was another hard thing about it all. A young girl in trouble needs the soothing solace and support and sympathy of persons of her own sex, and the delicate offices and gentle ministries which only these can furnish; yet in all these months of gloomy captivity in her dungeon Joan never saw the face of a girl or a woman. Think how her heart would have leaped to see such a face.

Consider. If you would realize how great Joan of Arc was, remember that it was out of such a place and such circumstances that she came week after week and month after month and confronted the master intellects of France single-handed, and baffled their cunningest schemes, defeated their ablest plans, detected and avoided their secretest traps and pitfalls, broke their lines, repelled their assaults, and camped on the field after every engagement; steadfast always, true to her faith and her ideals; defying torture, defying the stake, and answering threats of eternal death and the pains of hell with a simple "Let come what may, here I take my stand and will abide."

Yes, if you would realize how great was the soul, how profound the wisdom, and how luminous the intellect of Joan of Arc, you must study her there, where she fought out that long fight all alone — and not merely against the subtlest brains and deepest learning of France, but against the ignoblest deceits, the meanest treacheries, and the hardest hearts to be found in any land, pagan or Christian.

She was great in battle — we all know that; great in foresight; great in loyalty and patriotism; great in persuading discontented chiefs and reconciling conflicting interests and passions; great in the ability to discover merit and genius wherever it lay hidden; great in picturesque and eloquent speech; supremely great in the gift of firing the hearts of hopeless men with noble enthusiasms, the gift of turning hares into heroes, slaves and skulkers into battalions that march to death with songs upon their lips. But all these are exalting activities; they keep hand and heart and brain keyed up to their work: there is the joy of achievement, the inspiration of stir and movement, the applause which hails success; the soul is overflowing with life and energy, the faculties are at white heat; weariness, despondency, inertia — these do not exist.

Yes, Joan of Arc was great always, great everywhere, but she was greatest in the Rouen trials. There she rose above the limitations and infirmities of our human nature, and accomplished under blighting and unnerving and hopeless conditions all that her splendid equipment of moral and intellectual forces could have accomplished if they had been supplemented by the mighty helps of hope and cheer and light, the presence of friendly faces, and a fair and equal fight, with the great world looking on and wondering.

CHAPTER XVIII.

TOWARD the end of the ten-day interval the University of Paris rendered its decision concerning the Twelve Articles. By this finding, Joan was guilty upon all the counts: she must renounce her errors and make satisfaction, or be abandoned to the secular arm for punishment.

The University's mind was probably already made up before the Articles were laid before it; yet it took it from the fifth to the eighteenth to produce its verdict. I think the delay may have been caused by temporary difficulties concerning two points:

1, As to who the fiends were who were represented in Joan's Voices;

2, As to whether her saints spoke French only.

You understand, the University decided emphatically that it was fiends who spoke in those Voices; it would need to prove that, and it did. It found out who the fiends were, and named them in the verdict: Belial, Satan, and Behemoth. This has always seemed a doubtful thing to me, and not entitled to much credit. I think so for this reason: if the University had actually known it was those three, it would for very consistency's sake have told *how* it knew it, and not stopped with the mere assertion, since it had made Joan explain how she knew they were *not* fiends. Does not that seem reasonable? To my mind the University's position was weak, and I will tell you why. It had claimed that Joan's angels were devils in disguise, and we all know that devils do disguise themselves as angels; up to that point the University's position was strong; but you see yourself that it eats it own argument when it turns around and pretends that *it* can tell who such apparitions are, while denying the like ability to a person with as good a head on her shoulders as the best one the University could produce.

The doctors of the University had to see those creatures in order to know; and if Joan was deceived, it is argument that they in their turn could also be deceived, for their insight and judgment were surely not clearer than hers.

As to the other point which I have thought may have proved a difficulty and cost the University delay, I will touch but a moment upon that, and pass on. The University decided that it was blasphemy for Joan to say that her saints spoke French and not English, and were on the French side in political sympathies. I think that the thing which troubled the doctors of theology was this: they had decided that the three Voices were Satan and two other devils; but they had also decided that these Voices were *not* on the French side — thereby tacitly asserting that they were on the English side; and if on the English side, then they must be angels and not devils. Otherwise, the situation was embarrassing. You see, the University being the wisest and deepest and most erudite body in the world, it would like to be logical if it could, for the sake of its reputation; therefore it would study and study, days and days, trying to find some good common-sense reason for proving the Voices devils in Article No. 1 and proving them angels in Article No. 10. However, they had to give it up. They found no way out; and so, to this day, the University's verdict remains just so—devils in No. 1, angels in No. 10; and no way to reconcile the discrepancy.

The envoys brought the verdict to Rouen, and with it a letter for Cauchon which was full of fervid praise. The University complimented him on his zeal in hunting down this woman "whose venom had infected the faithful of the whole West," and as recompense it as good as promised him "a crown of imperishable glory in heaven." Only *that!* —a crown in heaven; a promissory note and no indorser; always something away off yonder; not a word about the Archbishopric of Rouen, which was the thing Cauchon was destroying his soul for. A crown in heaven; it must have sounded like a sarcasm to him, after all his hard work. What should *he* do in heaven? he did not know anybody there.

On the nineteenth of May a court of fifty judges sat in the archiepiscopal palace to discuss Joan's fate. A few wanted her delivered over to the secular arm at once for punishment, but the rest insisted that she be once more "charitably admonished" first.

So the same court met in the castle on the twenty-third, and Joan was brought to the bar. Pierre Maurice, a canon of Rouen, made a speech to Joan in which he admonished her to save her life and her soul by renouncing her errors and surrendering to the Church. He finished with a stern threat: if she remained obstinate the damnation of her soul was certain, the destruction of her body probable. But Joan was immovable. She said:

"If I were under sentence, and saw the fire before me, and the executioner ready to light it—more, if I were in the fire itself, I would say none but the things which I have said in these trials; and I would abide by them till I died."

A deep silence followed now, which endured some moments. It lay upon me like a weight. I knew it for an omen. Then Cauchon, grave and solemn, turned to Pierre Maurice:

"Have you anything further to say?"

The priest bowed low, and said:

"Nothing, my lord."

"Prisoner at the bar, have you anything further to say?"

"Nothing."

"Then the debate is closed. To-morrow, sentence will be pronounced. Remove the prisoner."

She seemed to go from the place erect and noble. But I do not know; my sight was dim with tears.

To-morrow — twenty-fourth of May! Exactly a year since I saw her go speeding across the plain at the head of her troops, her silver helmet shining, her silvery cape fluttering in the wind, her white plumes flowing, her sword held aloft; saw her charge the Burgundian camp three times, and carry it; saw her wheel to the right and spur for the duke's reserves; saw her fling herself against it in the last assault she was ever to make. And now that fatal day was come again — and see what it was bringing!

CHAPTER XIX.

JOAN had been adjudged guilty of heresy, sorcery, and all the other terrible crimes set forth in the Twelve Articles, and her life was in Cauchon's hands at last. He could send her to the stake at once. His work was finished now, you think? He was satisfied? Not at all. What would his Archbishopric be worth if the people should get the idea into their heads that this faction of interested priests, slaving under the English lash, had wrongly condemned and burned Joan of Arc, Deliverer of France? That would be to make of her a holy martyr. Then her spirit would rise from her body's ashes, a thousand-fold re-enforced, and sweep the English domination into the sea, and Cauchon along with it. No, the victory was not complete yet. Joan's guilt must be established by evidence which would satisfy the people. Where was that evidence to be found? There was only one person in the world who could furnish it — *Joan of Arc herself.* She must condemn herself, and in public — at least she must *seem* to do it.

But how was this to be managed? Weeks had

been spent already in trying to get her to surrender — time wholly wasted; what was to persuade her now? Torture had been threatened, the fire had been threatened; what was left? Illness, deadly fatigue, and the sight of the fire, the presence of the fire! That was left.

Now that was a shrewd thought. She was but a girl after all, and, under illness and exhaustion, subject to a girl's weaknesses.

Yes, it was shrewdly thought. She had tacitly said herself that under the bitter pains of the rack they would be able to extort a false confession from her. It was a hint worth remembering, and it was remembered.

She had furnished another hint at the same time: that as soon as the pains were gone, she would retract the confession. That hint was also remembered.

She had herself taught them what to do, you see. First, they must wear out her strength, then frighten her with the fire. Second, while the fright was on her, she must be made to sign a paper.

But she would demand a reading of the paper. They could not venture to refuse this, with the public there to hear. Suppose that during the reading her courage should return? she would refuse to sign then. Very well, even that difficulty could be got over. They could read a short paper of no importance, then slip a long and deadly one into its place and trick her into signing *that*.

Yet there was still one other difficulty. If they made her seem to abjure, that would free her from the death penalty. They could keep her in a prison of the Church, but they could not kill her. That would not answer; for only her death would content the English. Alive she was a terror, in a prison or out of it. She had escaped from two prisons already.

But even that difficulty could be managed. Cauchon would make promises to her; in return she would promise to leave off the male dress. He would violate his promises, and that would so situate her that she would not be able to keep hers. Her lapse would condemn her to the stake, and the stake would be ready.

These were the several moves; there was nothing to do but to make them, each in its order, and the game was won. One might almost name the day that the betrayed girl, the most innocent creature in France and the noblest, would go to her pitiful death.

And the time was favorable — cruelly favorable. Joan's spirit had as yet suffered no decay, it was as sublime and masterful as ever; but her body's forces had been steadily wasting away in those last ten days, and a strong mind needs a healthy body for its rightful support.

The world knows now that Cauchon's plan was as I have sketched it to you, but the world did not know it at that time. There are sufficient indications that Warwick and all the other English chiefs except the highest one—the Cardinal of Winchester—were not let into the secret; also, that only Loyseleur and Beaupere, on the French side, knew the scheme. Sometimes I have doubted if even Loyseleur and Beaupere knew the whole of it at first. However, if any did, it was these two.

It is usual to let the condemned pass their last night of life in peace, but this grace was denied to poor Joan, if one may credit the rumors of the time. Loyseleur was smuggled into her presence, and in the character of priest, friend, and secret partisan of France and hater of England, he spent some hours in beseeching her to do "the only right and righteous thing"—submit to the Church, as a good Christian should; and that then she would straightway get out of the clutches of the dreaded English and be transferred to the Church's prison, where she would be honorably used and have women about her for jailers. He knew where to touch her. He knew how odious to her was the presence of her rough and profane English guards; he knew that her Voices had vaguely promised something which she interpreted to be escape, rescue, release of some sort, and the chance to burst upon France once more and victoriously complete the great work which she had been commissioned of Heaven to do. Also there was that other thing: if her failing body could be further weakened by loss of rest and sleep now, her tired mind would be dazed and drowsy on the morrow, and in ill condition to stand out against persuasions, threats, and the sight of the stake, and also be purblind to traps and snares which it would be swift to detect when in its normal estate.

I do not need to tell you that there was no rest for me that night. Nor for Noël. We went to the main gate of the city before nightfall, with a hope in our minds, based upon that vague prophecy of Joan's Voices which seemed to promise a rescue by force at the last moment. The immense news had flown swiftly far and wide that at last Joan of Arc was condemned, and would be sentenced and burned alive on the morrow; and so crowds of people were flowing in at the gate, and other crowds were being refused admission by the soldiery; these being people who brought doubtful passes or none at all. We scanned these crowds eagerly, but there was nothing about them to indicate that they were our old war-comrades in disguise, and certainly there were no familiar faces among them. And so, when the gate was closed at last, we turned away grieved, and more disappointed than we cared to admit, either in speech or thought.

The streets were surging tides of excited men. It was difficult to make one's way. Toward midnight our aimless tramp brought us to the neighborhood of the beautiful church of St. Ouen, and there all was bustle and work. The square was a wilderness of torches and people; and through a guarded passage dividing the pack, laborers were carrying planks and timbers and disappearing with them through the gate of the churchyard. We asked what was going forward; the answer was:

"Scaffolds and the stake. Don't you know that the French witch is to be burned in the morning?"

Then we went away. We had no heart for that place.

At dawn we were at the city gate again; this time with a hope which our wearied bodies and fevered minds magnified into a large probability. We had heard a report that the Abbot of Jumièges with all his monks was coming to witness the burning. Our desire, abetted by our imagination, turned those nine hundred monks into Joan's old campaigners, and their Abbot into La Hire or the Bastard or D'Alençon; and we watched them file in, unchallenged, the multitude respectfully dividing and uncovering while they passed, with our hearts in our throats and our eyes swimming with tears of joy and pride and exultation; and we tried to catch glimpses of the faces under the cowls, and were prepared to give signal to any recognized face that we were Joan's men and ready and eager to kill and be killed in the good cause. How foolish we were; but we were young, you know, and youth hopeth all things, believeth all things.

CHAPTER XX.

IN the morning I was at my official post. It was on a platform raised the height of a man, in the churchyard, under the eaves of St. Ouen. On this same platform was a crowd of priests and important citizens, and several lawyers. Abreast it, with a small space between, was another and larger platform, handsomely canopied against sun and rain, and richly carpeted; also it was furnished with comfortable chairs, and with two which were more sumptuous than the others, and raised above the general level. One of these two was occupied by a prince of the royal blood of England, his Eminence the Cardinal of Winchester; the other by Cauchon, Bishop of Beauvais. In the rest of the chairs sat three bishops, the Vice-Inquisitor, eight abbots, and the sixty-two friars and lawyers who had sat as Joan's judges in her late trials.

Twenty steps in front of the platforms was another — a table-topped pyramid of stone, built up in retreating courses, thus forming steps. Out of this rose that grisly thing, the stake; about the stake bundles of fagots and firewood were piled. On the ground at the base of the pyramid stood three crimson figures, the executioner and his assistants. At their feet lay what had been a goodly heap of brands, but was now a smokeless nest of ruddy coals; a foot or two from this was a supplemental supply of wood and fagots compacted into a pile shoulder-high and containing as much as six pack-horse loads. Think of that. We seem so delicately made, so destructible, so insubstantial; yet it is easier to reduce a granite statue to ashes than it is to do that with a man's body.

The sight of the stake sent physical pains tingling down the nerves of my body; and yet, turn as I would, my eyes would keep coming back to it, such fascination has the grewsome and the terrible for us.

The space occupied by the platforms and the stake was kept open by a wall of English soldiery, standing elbow to elbow, erect and stalwart figures, fine and sightly in their polished steel; while from behind them on every hand stretched far away a level plain of human heads; and there was no window and no housetop within our view, howsoever distant, but was black with patches and masses of people.

But there was no noise, no stir; it was as if the world was dead. The impressiveness of this silence and solemnity was deepened by a leaden twilight, for the sky was hidden by a pall of low-hanging storm-clouds; and above the remote horizon faint winkings of heat-lightning played, and now and then one caught the dull mutterings and complainings of distant thunder.

At last the stillness was broken. From beyond the square rose an indistinct sound, but familiar — curt, crisp phrases of command; next I saw the plain of heads dividing, and the steady swing of a marching host was glimpsed between. My heart leaped for a moment. Was it La Hire and his hellions? No — that was not their gait. No, it was the prisoner and her escort; it was Joan of Arc, under guard, that was coming; my spirits sank as low as they had been before. Weak as she was they made her walk; they would increase her weakness all they could. The distance was not great — it was but a few hundred yards — but short as it was it was a heavy tax upon one who had been lying chained in one spot for months, and whose feet had lost their powers from inaction. Yes, and for a year Joan had known only the cool damps of a dungeon, and now she was dragging herself through this sultry summer heat, this airless and suffocating void. As she entered the gate, drooping with exhaustion, there was that creature Loyseleur at her side with his head bent to her ear. We knew afterward that he had been with her again this morning in the prison wearying her with his persuasions and enticing her with false promises, and that he was now still at the same work at the gate, imploring her to yield everything that would be required of her, and assuring her that if she would do this all would be well with her: she would be rid of the dreaded English and find safety in the powerful shelter and protection of the Church. A miserable man, a stony-hearted man!

The moment Joan was seated on the platform she closed her eyes and allowed her chin to fall; and so sat, with her hands nestling in her lap, indifferent to everything, caring for nothing but rest. And she was so white again — white as alabaster.

How the faces of that packed mass of humanity lighted up with interest, and with what intensity all eyes gazed upon this fragile girl! And how natural it was; for these people realized that at last they were looking upon that person whom they had so long hungered to see; a person whose name and fame filled all Europe, and made all other names and all other renowns insignificant by comparison: Joan of Arc, the wonder of the time, and destined to be the wonder of all times! And I could read as by print, in their marveling countenances, the words that were drifting through their minds: "Can it be true; is it believable, that it is this little creature, this girl, this child with the good face, the sweet face, the beautiful face, the dear and bonny face, that has carried fortresses by storm, charged at the head of victorious armies, blown the might of England out of her path with a breath, and fought a long campaign, solitary and alone, against the massed brains and learning of France — and had won it if the fight had been fair!"

Evidently Cauchon had grown afraid of Manchon

because of his pretty apparent leanings toward Joan, for another recorder was in the chief place here, which left my master and me nothing to do but sit idle and look on.

Well, I supposed that everything had been done which could be thought of to tire Joan's body and mind, but it was a mistake; one more device had been invented. This was to preach a long sermon to her in that oppressive heat.

When the preacher began, she cast up one distressed and disappointed look, then dropped her head again. This preacher was Guillaume Erard, an oratorical celebrity. He got his text from the Twelve Lies. He emptied upon Joan all the calumnies in detail that had been bottled up in that mess of venom, and called her all the brutal names that the Twelve were labeled with, working himself into a whirlwind of fury as he went on; but his labors were wasted, she seemed lost in dreams, she made no sign, she did not seem to hear. At last he launched this apostrophe:

"O France, how hast thou been abused! Thou hast always been the home of Christianity; but now, Charles, who calls himself thy King and governor, indorses, like the heretic and schismatic that he is, the words and deeds of a worthless and infamous woman!" Joan raised her head, and her eyes began to burn and flash. The preacher turned toward her: "It is to you, Joan, that I speak, and I tell you that your King is schismatic and a heretic!"

Ah, he might abuse *her* to his heart's content; she could endure that; but to her dying moment she could never hear in patience a word against that ingrate, that treacherous dog our King, whose proper place was here, at this moment, sword in hand, routing these reptiles and saving this most noble servant that ever King had in this world — and he *would* have been there if he had not been what I have called him. Joan's loyal soul was outraged, and she turned upon the preacher and flung out a few words with a spirit which the crowd recognized as being in accordance with the Joan of Arc traditions:

"By my faith, sir! I make bold to say and swear, on pain of death, that he is the most noble Christian of all Christians, and the best lover of the faith and the Church!"

There was an explosion of applause from the crowd — which angered the preacher, for he had been aching long to hear an expression like this, and now that it was come at last it had fallen to the wrong person: he had done all the work; the other had carried off all the spoil. He stamped his foot and shouted to the sheriff:

"Make her shut up!"

That made the crowd laugh.

A mob has small respect for a grown man who has to call on a sheriff to protect him from a sick girl.

Joan had damaged the preacher's cause more with

one sentence than he had helped it with a hundred; so he was much put out, and had trouble to get a good start again. But he needn't have bothered; there was no occasion. It was mainly an English-feeling mob. It had but obeyed a law of our nature — an irresistible law — to enjoy and applaud a spirited and promptly delivered retort, no matter who makes it. The mob was with the preacher; it had been beguiled for a moment, but only that; it would soon return. It was there to see this girl burnt; so that it got that satisfaction — without too much delay — it would be content.

Presently the preacher formally summoned Joan to submit to the Church. He made the demand with confidence, for he had gotten the idea from Loyseleur and Beaupere that she was worn to the bone, exhausted, and would not be able to put forth any more resistance; and, indeed, to look at her it seemed that they must be right. Nevertheless, she made one more effort to hold her ground, and said, wearily:

"As to that matter, I have answered my judges before. I have told them to report all that I have said and done to our holy Father the Pope — to whom, and to God first, I appeal."

Again, out of her native wisdom, she had brought those words of tremendous import, but was ignorant of their value. But they could have availed her nothing in any case now, with the stake there and these thousands of enemies about her. Yet they made every churchman there blench, and the preacher changed the subject with all haste. Well might those criminals blench, for Joan's appeal of her case to the Pope stripped Cauchon at once of jurisdiction over it, and annulled all that he and his judges had already done in the matter and all that they should do in it thenceforth.

Joan went on presently to reiterate, after some further talk, that she had acted by command of God in her deeds and utterances; then, when an attempt was made to implicate the King, and friends of hers and his, she stopped that. She said:

"I charge my deeds and words upon no one, neither upon my King nor any other. If there is any fault in them, I am responsible and no other."

She was asked if she would not recant those of her words and deeds which had been pronounced evil by her judges. Her answer made confusion and damage again:

"I submit them to God and the Pope."

The Pope once more! It was very embarrassing. Here was a person who was asked to submit her case to the Church, and who frankly consents—offers to submit it to the very head of it. What more could any one require? How was one to answer such a formidably unanswerable answer as that?

The worried judges put their heads together and whispered and planned and discussed. Then they brought forth this sufficiently shambling conclusion

—but it was the best they could do, in so close a place: they said the Pope was so far away; and it was not necessary to go to him anyway, because these present judges had sufficient power and authority to deal with the present case, and were in effect "the Church" to that extent. At another time they could have smiled at this conceit, but not now; they were not comfortable enough now.

The mob was getting impatient. It was beginning to put on a threatening aspect; it was tired of standing, tired of the scorching heat; and the thunder was coming nearer, the lightning was flashing brighter. It was necessary to hurry this matter to a close. Erard showed Joan a written form, which had been prepared and made all ready beforehand, and asked her to abjure.

"Abjure? What is abjure?"

She did not know the word. It was explained to her by Massieu. She tried to understand, but she was breaking, under exhaustion, and she could not gather the meaning. It was all a jumble and confusion of strange words. In her despair she sent out this beseeching cry:

"I appeal to the Church universal whether I ought to abjure or no!"

Erard exclaimed:

"You shall abjure instantly, or instantly be burnt!"

She glanced up, at those awful words, and for the first time she saw the stake and the mass of red coals—redder and angrier than ever now under the constantly deepening storm-gloom. She gasped and staggered up out of her seat muttering and mumbling incoherently, and gazed vacantly upon the people and the scene about her like one who is dazed, or thinks he dreams, and does not know where he is.

The priests crowded about her imploring her to sign the paper, there were many voices beseeching and urging her at once, there was great turmoil and shouting and excitement among the populace and everywhere.

"Sign! sign!" from the priests; "sign—sign and be saved!" And Loyseleur was urging at her ear, "Do as I told you—do not destroy yourself!"

Joan said plaintively to these people:

"Ah, you do not do well to seduce me."

The judges joined their voices to the others. Yes, even the iron in *their* hearts melted, and they said:

"O Joan, we pity you so! Take back what you have said, or we must deliver you up to punishment."

And now there was another voice—it was from the other platform—pealing solemnly above the din: Cauchon's—reading the sentence of death!

Joan's strength was all spent. She stood looking about her in a bewildered way a moment, then slowly she sank to her knees, and bowed her head and said:

"I submit."

They gave her no time to reconsider — they knew the peril of that. The moment the words were out of her mouth Massieu was reading to her the abjuration, and she was repeating the words after him mechanically, unconsciously — and *smiling;* for her wandering mind was far away in some happier world.

Then this short paper of six lines was slipped aside and a long one of many pages was smuggled into its place, and she, noting nothing, put her mark to it, saying, in pathetic apology, that she did not know how to write. But a secretary of the King of England was there to take care of that defect; he guided her hand with his own, and wrote her name — *Jehanne.*

The great crime was accomplished. She had signed — what? She did not know — but the others knew. She had signed a paper confessing herself a sorceress, a dealer with devils, a liar, a blasphemer of God and His angels, a lover of blood, a promoter of sedition, cruel, wicked, commissioned of Satan; and this signature of her bound her to resume the dress of a woman. There were other promises, but that one would answer, without the others; that one could be made to destroy her.

Loyseleur pressed forward and praised her for having done "such a good day's work."

But she was still dreamy, she hardly heard.

Then Cauchon pronounced the words which dissolved the excommunication and restored her to her beloved Church, with all the dear privileges of worship. Ah, she heard that! You could see it in the deep gratitude that rose in her face and transfigured it with joy.

But how transient was that happiness! For Cauchon, without a tremor of pity in his voice, added these crushing words:

"And that she may repent of her crimes and repeat them no more, she is sentenced to perpetual imprisonment, with the bread of affliction and the water of anguish!"

Perpetual imprisonment! She had never dreamed of that—such a thing had never been hinted to her by Loyseleur or by any other. Loyseleur had distinctly said and promised that "all would be well with her." And the very last words spoken to her by Erard, on that very platform, when he was urging her to abjure, was a straight, unqualified promise—that if she would do it she should *go free from captivity*.

She stood stunned and speechless a moment; then she remembered, with such solacement as the thought could furnish, that by another clear promise—a promise made by Cauchon himself—she would at least be the Church's captive, and have women about her in place of a brutal foreign soldiery. So she turned to the body of priests and said, with a sad resignation:

"Now, you men of the Church, take me to your prison, and leave me no longer in the hands of the

English;" and she gathered up her chains and prepared to move.

But alas! now came these shameful words from Cauchon — and with them a mocking laugh:

"Take her to the prison whence she came!"

Poor abused girl! She stood dumb, smitten, paralyzed. It was pitiful to see. She had been beguiled, lied to, betrayed; she saw it all now.

The rumbling of a drum broke upon the stillness, and for just one moment she thought of the glorious deliverance promised by her Voices — I read it in the rapture that lit her face; then she saw what it was — her prison escort — and that light faded, never to revive again. And now her head began a piteous rocking motion, swaying slowly, this way and that, as is the way when one is suffering unwordable pain, or when one's heart is broken; then drearily she went from us, with her face in her hands, and sobbing bitterly.

CHAPTER XXI.

THERE is no certainty that any one in all Rouen was in the secret of the deep game which Cauchon was playing except the Cardinal of Winchester. Then you can imagine the astonishment and stupefaction of that vast mob gathered there and those crowds of churchmen assembled on the two platforms, when they saw Joan of Arc moving away, alive and whole — slipping out of their grip at last, after all this tedious waiting, all this tantalizing expectancy.

Nobody was able to stir or speak for a while, so paralyzing was the universal astonishment, so unbelievable the fact that the stake was actually standing there unoccupied and its prey gone. Then suddenly everybody broke into a fury of rage; maledictions and charges of treachery began to fly freely; yes, and even stones: a stone came near killing the Cardinal of Winchester — it just missed his head. But the man who threw it was not to blame, for he was excited, and a person who is excited never can throw straight.

The tumult was very great, indeed, for a while.

In the midst of it a chaplain of the Cardinal even forgot the proprieties so far as to opprobriously assail the august Bishop of Beauvais himself, shaking his fist in his face and shouting:

"By God, you are a traitor!"

"You lie!" responded the Bishop.

He a traitor! Oh, far from it; he certainly was the last Frenchman that any Briton had a right to bring that charge against.

The Earl of Warwick lost his temper, too. He was a doughty soldier, but when it came to the intellectuals—when it came to delicate chicane, and scheming, and trickery—he couldn't see any further through a millstone than another. So he burst out in his frank warrior fashion, and swore that the King of England was being treacherously used, and that Joan of Arc was going to be allowed to cheat the stake. But they whispered comfort into his ear:

"Give yourself no uneasiness, my lord; we shall soon have her again."

Perhaps the like tidings found their way all around, for good news travels fast as well as bad. At any rate the ragings presently quieted down, and the huge concourse crumbled apart and disappeared. And thus we reached the noon of that fearful Thursday.

We two youths were happy; happier than any words can tell—for we were not in the secret any more than the rest. Joan's life was saved. We knew that, and that was enough. France would hear of this day's infamous work—and then! Why, then her gallant sons would flock to her standard by thousands and thousands, multitudes upon multitudes, and their wrath would be like the wrath of the ocean when the storm-winds sweep it; and they would hurl themselves against this doomed city and overwhelm it like the resistless tides of that ocean, and Joan of Arc would march again! In six days—seven days—one short week—noble France, grateful France, indignant France, would be thundering at these gates—let us count the hours, let us count the minutes, let us count the seconds! O happy day, O day of ecstasy, how our hearts sang in our bosoms!

For we were young, then; yes, we were very young.

Do you think the exhausted prisoner was allowed to rest and sleep after she had spent the small remnant of her strength in dragging her tired body back to the dungeon?

No; there was no rest for her, with those sleuth-hounds on her track. Cauchon and some of his people followed her to her lair straightway; they found her dazed and dull, her mental and physical forces in a state of prostration. They told her she had abjured; that she had made certain promises—among them, to resume the apparel of her sex; and that if she relapsed, the Church would cast her out for good and all. She heard the words, but they had no meaning to her. She was like a person who has taken a narcotic and is dying for sleep, dying for rest from nagging, dying to be let alone, and who mechanically does everything the persecutor asks, taking but dull note of the things done, and but dully recording them in the memory. And so Joan put on the gown which Cauchon and his people had brought; and would come to herself by and by, and have at first but a dim idea as to when and how the change had come about.

Cauchon went away happy and content. Joan had resumed woman's dress without protest; also she had been formally warned against relapsing. He had witnesses to these facts. How could matters be better?

But suppose she should *not* relapse?

Why, then she must be forced to do it.

Did Cauchon hint to the English guards that thenceforth if they chose to make their prisoner's captivity crueler and bitterer than ever, no official notice would be taken of it? Perhaps so; since the guards did begin that policy at once, and no official notice *was* taken of it. Yes, from that moment Joan's life in that dungeon was made almost unendurable. Do not ask me to enlarge upon it. I will not do it.

CHAPTER XXII.

FRIDAY and Saturday were happy days for Noël and me. Our minds were full of our splendid dream of France aroused — France shaking her mane — France on the march — France at the gates — Rouen in ashes, and Joan free! Our imagination was on fire; we were delirious with pride and joy. For we were very young, as I have said.

We knew nothing about what had been happening in the dungeon the yester-afternoon. We supposed that as Joan had abjured and been taken back into the forgiving bosom of the Church, she was being gently used now, and her captivity made as pleasant and comfortable for her as the circumstances would allow. So, in high contentment, we planned out our share in the great rescue, and fought our part of the fight over and over again during those two happy days — as happy days as ever I have known.

Sunday morning came. I was awake, enjoying the balmy, lazy weather, and thinking. Thinking of the rescue — what else? I had no other thought now. I was absorbed in that, drunk with the happiness of it.

I heard a voice shouting far down the street, and soon it came nearer, and I caught the words:

"*Joan of Arc has relapsed! The witch's time has come!*"

It stopped my heart, it turned my blood to ice. That was more than sixty years ago, but that triumphant note rings as clear in my memory to-day as it rang in my ear that long-vanished summer morning. We are so strangely made; the memories that could make us happy pass away; it is the memories that break our hearts that abide.

Soon other voices took up that cry — tens, scores, hundreds of voices; all the world seemed filled with the brutal joy of it. And there were other clamors — the clatter of rushing feet, merry congratulations, bursts of coarse laughter, the rolling of drums, the boom and crash of distant bands profaning the sacred day with the music of victory and thanksgiving.

About the middle of the afternoon came a summons for Manchon and me to go to Joan's dungeon — a summons from Cauchon. But by that time distrust had already taken possession of the English and their soldiery again, and all Rouen was in an angry and threatening mood. We could see plenty of evidences of this from our own windows — fist-shaking, black looks, tumultuous tides of furious men billowing by along the street.

And we learned that up at the castle things were going very badly, indeed; that there was a great mob gathered there who considered the relapse a lie and a priestly trick, and among them many half-drunk English soldiers. Moreover, these people had gone beyond words. They had laid hands upon a number of churchmen who were trying to enter the castle, and it had been difficult work to rescue them and save their lives.

And so Manchon refused to go. He said he would not go a step without a safeguard from Warwick. So next morning Warwick sent an escort of soldiers, and then we went. Matters had not grown peacefuler meantime, but worse. The soldiers protected us from bodily damage, but as we passed through the great mob at the castle we were assailed with insults and shameful epithets. I bore it well enough, though, and said to myself, with secret satisfaction, "In three or four short days, my lads, you will be employing your tongues in a different sort from this — and I shall be there to hear."

To my mind these were as good as dead men. How many of them would still be alive after the rescue that was coming? Not more than enough to amuse the executioner a short half-hour, certainly.

It turned out that the report was true. Joan had relapsed. She was sitting there in her chains, clothed again in her male attire.

She accused nobody. That was her way. It was not in her character to hold a servant to account for what his master had made him do, and her mind had cleared now, and she knew that the advantage which had been taken of her the previous morning had its origin, not in the subordinate, but in the master — Cauchon.

Here is what had happened. While Joan slept, in the early morning of Sunday, one of the guards stole her female apparel and put her male attire in its place. When she woke she asked for the other dress, but the guards refused to give it back. She protested, and said she was forbidden to wear the male dress. But they continued to refuse. She had to have clothing, for modesty's sake; moreover, she saw that she could not save her life if she must fight for it against treacheries like this; so she put on the forbidden garments, knowing what the end would be. She was weary of the struggle, poor thing.

We had followed in the wake of Cauchon, the Vice-Inquisitor, and the others — six or eight — and when I saw Joan sitting there, despondent, forlorn, and still in chains, when I was expecting to find her situation so different, I did not know what to make of it. The shock was very great. I had doubted the relapse perhaps; possibly I had believed in it, but had not realized it.

Cauchon's victory was complete. He had had a harassed and irritated and disgusted look for a long time, but that was all gone now, and contentment and serenity had taken its place. His purple face was full of tranquil and malicious happiness. He went trailing his robes and stood grandly in front of Joan, with his legs apart, and remained so more than a minute, gloating over her and enjoying the sight of this poor ruined creature, who had won so lofty a place for him in the service of the meek and merciful Jesus, Saviour of the World, Lord of the Universe—in case England kept her promise to him, who kept no promises himself.

Presently the judges began to question Joan. One of them, named Marguerie, who was a man with more insight than prudence, remarked upon Joan's change of clothing, and said:

"There is something suspicious about this. How could it have come about without connivance on the part of others? Perhaps even something worse?"

"Thousand devils!" screamed Cauchon, in a fury. "Will you shut your mouth?"

"Armagnac! Traitor!" shouted the soldiers on guard, and made a rush for Marguerie with their lances leveled. It was with the greatest difficulty that he was saved from being run through the body. He made no more attempts to help the inquiry, poor man. The other judges proceeded with the questionings.

"Why have you resumed this male habit?"

I did not quite catch her answer, for just then a soldier's halberd slipped from his fingers and fell on the stone floor with a crash; but I thought I understood Joan to say that she had resumed it of her own motion.

"But you have promised and sworn that you would not go back to it."

I was full of anxiety to hear her answer to that question; and when it came it was just what I was expecting. She said — quite quietly:

"I have never intended and never understood myself to swear I would not resume it."

There — I had been sure, all along, that she did not know what she was doing and saying on the platform Thursday, and this answer of hers was proof that I had not been mistaken. Then she went on to add this:

"But I had a right to resume it, because the promises made to me have not been kept — promises that I should be allowed to go to mass and receive the communion, and that I should be freed from the bondage of these chains — but they are still upon me, as you see."

"Nevertheless, you have abjured, and have especially promised to return no more to the dress of a man."

Then Joan held out her fettered hands sorrowfully toward these unfeeling men and said:

"I would rather die than continue so. But if they may be taken off, and if I may hear mass, and be removed to a penitential prison, and have a woman about me, I will be good, and will do what shall seem good to you that I do."

Cauchon sniffed scoffingly at that. Honor the compact which he and his had made with her? Fulfill its conditions? What need of that? Conditions had been a good thing to concede, temporarily, and for advantage; but they had served their turn — let something of a fresher sort and of more consequence be considered. The resumption of the male dress was sufficient for all practical purposes, but perhaps Joan could be led to add something to that fatal crime. So Cauchon asked her if her Voices had spoken to her since Thursday — and he reminded her of her abjuration.

"Yes," she answered; and then it came out that the Voices had talked with her about the abjuration — *told* her about it, I suppose. She guilelessly re-asserted the heavenly origin of her mission, and did it with the untroubled mien of one who was not conscious that she had ever knowingly repudiated it. So I was convinced once more that she had had no notion of what she was doing that Thursday morning on the platform. Finally she said, "My Voices told me I did very wrong to confess that what I had done was not well." Then she sighed, and said with simplicity, "But it was the fear of the fire that made me do so."

That is, fear of the fire had made her sign a paper whose contents she had not understood then, but understood now by revelation of her Voices and by testimony of her persecutors.

She was sane now and not exhausted; her courage had come back, and with it her inborn loyalty to the truth. She was bravely and serenely speaking it again, knowing that it would deliver her body up to that very fire which had such terrors for her.

That answer of hers was quite long, quite frank, wholly free from concealments or palliations. It made me shudder; I knew she was pronouncing sentence of death upon herself. So did poor Manchon. And he wrote in the margin abreast of it:

RESPONSIO MORTIFERA.

Fatal answer. Yes, all present knew that it was, indeed, a fatal answer. Then there fell a silence such as falls in a sick-room when the watchers by the dying draw a deep breath and say softly one to another, "All is over."

Here, likewise, all was over; but after some moments Cauchon, wishing to clinch this matter and make it final, put this question:

"Do you still believe that your Voices are St. Marguerite and St. Catherine?"

"Yes—and that they come from God."

"Yet you denied them on the scaffold?"

Then she made direct and clear affirmation that she had never had any intention to deny them; and that if—I noted the *if*—"if she had made some retractions and revocations on the scaffold it was from fear of the fire, and was a violation of the truth."

There it is again, you see. She certainly never knew what it was she had done on the scaffold until she was told of it afterward by these people and by her Voices.

And now she closed this most painful scene with these words; and there was a weary note in them that was pathetic:

"I would rather do my penance all at once; let me die. I cannot endure captivity any longer."

The spirit born for sunshine and liberty so longed for release that it would take it in any form, even that.

Several among the company of judges went from the place troubled and sorrowful, the others in another mood. In the court of the castle we found the Earl of Warwick and fifty English waiting, impatient for news. As soon as Cauchon saw them he shouted—*laughing*—think of a man destroying a friendless poor girl and then having the heart to laugh at it:

"Make yourselves comfortable—it's all over with her!"

CHAPTER XXIII.

THE young can sink into abysses of despondency, and it was so with Noël and me now; but the hopes of the young are quick to rise again, and it was so with ours. We called back that vague promise of the Voices, and said the one to the other that the glorious release was to happen at "the last moment"—"that other time was not the last moment, but this is; it will happen now; the King will come, La Hire will come, and with them our veterans, and behind them all France!" And so we were full of heart again, and could already hear, in fancy, that stirring music the clash of steel and the war-cries and the uproar of the onset, and in fancy see our prisoner free, her chains gone, her sword in her hand.

But this dream was to pass also, and come to nothing. Late at night, when Manchon came in, he said:

"I am come from the dungeon, and I have a message for you from that poor child."

A message to me! If he had been noticing I think he would have discovered me—discovered that my indifference concerning the prisoner was a pretense; for I was caught off my guard, and was so moved and so exalted to be so honored by her that I must have shown my feeling in my face and manner.

"A message for me, your reverence?"

"Yes. It is something she wishes done. She said she had noticed the young man who helps me, and that he had a good face; and did I think he would do a kindness for her? I said I knew you would, and asked her what it was, and she said a letter—would you write a letter to her mother? And I said you would. But I said I would do it myself, and gladly; but she said no, that my labors were heavy, and she thought the young man would not mind the doing of this service for one not able to do it for herself, she not knowing how to write. Then I would have sent for you, and at that the sadness vanished out of her face. Why, it was as if she was going to see a friend, poor friendless thing. But I was not permitted. I did my best, but the orders remain as strict as ever, the doors are closed against all but officials; as before, none but officials may speak to her. So I went back and told her, and she sighed, and was sad again. Now this is what she begs you to write to her mother. It is partly a strange message, and to me means nothing, but she said her mother would understand. You will 'convey her adoring love to her family and her village friends, and say there will be no rescue, for that this night—and it is the third time in the twelve-month, and is final—she has seen The Vision of the Tree.' "

"How strange!"

"Yes, it *is* strange, but that is what she said; and said her parents would understand. And for a little time she was lost in dreams and thinkings, and her lips moved, and I caught in her muttering these lines, which she said over two or three times, and they seemed to bring peace and contentment to her. I set them down, thinking they might have some connection with her letter and be useful; but it was not so; they were a mere memory, floating idly in a tired mind, and they have no meaning, at least no relevancy."

I took the piece of paper, and found what I knew I should find:

> "And when in exile wand'ring, we
> Shall fainting yearn for glimpse of thee,
> Oh, rise upon our sight!"

There was no hope any more. I knew it now. I knew that Joan's letter was a message to Noël and me, as well as to her family, and that its object was to banish vain hopes from our minds and tell us from her own mouth of the blow that was going to fall upon us, so that we, being her soldiers, would know it for a command to bear it as became us and her, and so submit to the will of God; and in thus obeying, find assuagement of our grief. It was like her, for she was always thinking of others, not of herself. Yes, her heart was sore for us; she could find time to think of us, the humblest of her servants, and try to soften our pain, lighten the burden of our troubles,— she that was drinking of the bitter waters; she that was walking in the Valley of the Shadow of Death.

I wrote the letter. You will know what it cost me, without my telling you. I wrote it with the same wooden stylus which had put upon parchment the first words ever dictated by Joan of Arc — that high summons to the English to vacate France, two years past, when she was a lass of seventeen; it had now set down the last ones which she was ever to dictate. Then I broke it. For the pen that had served Joan of Arc could not serve any that would come after her in this earth without abasement.

The next day, May 29th, Cauchon summoned his serfs, and forty-two responded. It is charitable to believe that the other twenty were ashamed to come. The forty-two pronounced her a relapsed heretic, and condemned her to be delivered over to the secular arm. Cauchon thanked them. Then he sent orders that Joan be conveyed the next morning to the place known as the Old Market; and that she be then delivered to the civil judge, and by the civil judge to the executioner. That meant that she would be burnt.

All the afternoon and evening of Tuesday, the 29th, the news was flying, and the people of the country-side flocking to Rouen to see the tragedy —

all, at least, who could prove their English sympathies and count upon admission. The press grew thicker and thicker in the streets, the excitement grew higher and higher. And now a thing was noticeable again which had been noticeable more than once before — that there was pity for Joan in the hearts of many of these people. Whenever she had been in great danger it had manifested itself, and now it was apparent again — manifest in a pathetic dumb sorrow which was visible in many faces.

Early the next morning, Wednesday, Martin Ladvenu and another friar were sent to Joan to prepare her for death; and Manchon and I went with them — a hard service for me. We tramped through the dim corridors, winding this way and that, and piercing ever deeper and deeper into that vast heart of stone, and at last we stood before Joan. But she did not know it. She sat with her hands in her lap and her head bowed, thinking, and her face was very sad. One might not know what she was thinking of. Of her home, and the peaceful pastures, and the friends she was no more to see? Of her wrongs, and her forsaken estate, and the cruelties which had been put upon her? Or was it of death — the death which she had longed for, and which was now so close? Or was it of the *kind* of death she must suffer? I hoped not; for she feared only one kind, and that one had for her unspeakable terrors. I believed she so feared that one that with her strong will she would shut the thought of it wholly out of her mind, and hope and believe that God would take pity on her and grant her an easier one; and so it might chance that the awful news which we were bringing might come as a surprise to her at last.

We stood silent awhile, but she was still unconscious of us, still deep in her sad musings and far away. Then Martin Ladvenu said, softly:

"Joan."

She looked up then, with a little start, and a wan smile, and said:

"Speak. Have you a message for me?"

"Yes, my poor child. Try to bear it. Do you think you can bear it?"

"Yes"—very softly, and her head drooped again.

"I am come to prepare you for death."

A faint shiver trembled through her wasted body. There was a pause. In the stillness we could hear our breathings. Then she said, still in that low voice:

"When will it be?"

The muffled notes of a tolling bell floated to our ears out of the distance.

"Now. The time is at hand."

That slight shiver passed again.

"It is so soon—ah, it is so soon!"

There was a long silence. The distant throbbings of the bell pulsed through it, and we stood motionless and listening. But it was broken at last:

"What death is it?"

"By fire!"

"Oh, I knew it, I knew it!" She sprang wildly to her feet, and wound her hands in her hair, and began to writhe and sob, oh, so piteously, and mourn and grieve and lament, and turn to first one and then another of us, and search our faces beseechingly, as hoping she might find help and friendliness there, poor thing—she that had never denied these to any creature, even her wounded enemy on the battle-field.

"Oh, cruel, cruel, to treat me so! And must my body, that has never been defiled, be consumed to-day and turned to ashes? Ah, sooner would I that my head were cut off seven times than suffer this woful death. I had the promise of the Church's prison when I submitted, and if I had but been there, and not left here in the hands of my enemies, this miserable fate had not befallen me. Oh, I appeal to God the Great Judge, against the injustice which has been done me."

There was none there that could endure it. They turned away, with the tears running down their faces. In a moment I was on my knees at her feet. At once she thought only of my danger, and bent and whispered in my ear: "Up!—do not peril yourself, good heart. There—God bless you always!" and I felt the quick clasp of her hand. Mine was the last hand she touched with hers in life. None saw it; history does not know of it or tell of it, yet it is truc, just as I have told it. The next moment she saw Cauchon coming, and she went and stood before him and reproached him, saying:

"Bishop, it is by you that I die!"

He was not shamed, not touched; but said, smoothly:

"Ah, be patient, Joan. You die because you have not kept your promise, but have returned to your sins."

"Alas," she said, "if you had put me in the Church's prison, and given me right and proper keepers, as you promised, this would not have happened. And for this I summon you to answer before God!"

Then Cauchon winced, and looked less placidly content than before, and he turned him about and went away.

Joan stood awhile musing. She grew calmer, but occasionally she wiped her eyes, and now and then sobs shook her body; but their violence was modifying now, and the intervals between them were growing longer. Finally she looked up and saw Pierre Maurice, who had come in with the Bishop, and she said to him:

"Master Peter, where shall I be this night?"

"Have you not good hope in God?"

"Yes—and by His grace I shall be in Paradise."

Now Martin Ladvenu heard her in confession; then she begged for the sacrament. But how grant the communion to one who had been publicly cut off from the Church, and was now no more entitled to its privileges than an unbaptized pagan? The brother could not do this, but he sent to Cauchon to inquire what he must do. All laws, human and divine, were alike to that man — he respected none of them. He sent back orders to grant Joan whatever she wished. Her last speech to him had reached his fears, perhaps; it could not reach his heart, for he had none.

The Eucharist was brought now to that poor soul that had yearned for it with such unutterable longing all these desolate months. It was a solemn moment. While we had been in the deeps of the prison, the public courts of the castle had been filling up with crowds of the humbler sort of men and women, who had learned what was going on in Joan's cell, and had come with softened hearts to do — they knew not what; to hear — they knew not what. We knew nothing of this, for they were out of our view. And there were other great crowds of the like caste gathered in masses outside the castle gates. And when the lights and the other accompaniments of the Sacrament passed by, coming to Joan in the prison, all those multitudes kneeled down and began to pray for her, and many wept; and when the solemn ceremony of the communion began in Joan's cell, out of the distance a moving sound was borne moaning to our ears — it was those invisible multitudes chanting the litany for a departing soul.

The fear of the fiery death was gone from Joan of Arc now, to come again no more, except for one fleeting instant — then it would pass, and serenity and courage would take its place and abide till the end.

CHAPTER XXIV.

AT nine o'clock the Maid of Orleans, Deliverer of France, went forth in the grace of her innocence and her youth to lay down her life for the country she loved with such devotion, and for the King that had abandoned her. She sat in the cart that is used only for felons. In one respect she was treated worse than a felon; for whereas she was on her way to be sentenced by the civil arm, she already bore her judgment inscribed in advance upon a miter-shaped cap which she wore:

HERETIC, RELAPSED, APOSTATE, IDOLATER.

In the cart with her sat the friar Martin Ladvenu and Maître Jean Massieu. She looked girlishly fair and sweet and saintly in her long white robe, and when a gush of sunlight flooded her as she emerged from the gloom of the prison and was yet for a moment still framed in the arch of the somber gate, the massed multitudes of poor folk murmured "A vision! a vision!" and sank to their knees praying, and many of the women weeping; and the moving invocation for the dying rose again, and was taken up and borne along, a majestic wave of sound, which accompanied the doomed, solacing and blessing her, all the sorrowful way to the place of death. "Christ have pity! Saint Margaret have pity! Pray for her, all ye saints, archangels, and blessed martyrs, pray for her! Saints and angels intercede for her! From thy wrath, good Lord, deliver her! O Lord God, save her! Have mercy on her, we beseech Thee, good Lord!"

It is just and true what one of the histories has said: "The poor and the helpless had nothing but their prayers to give Joan of Arc; but these we may believe were not unavailing. There are few more pathetic events recorded in history than this weeping, helpless, praying crowd, holding their lighted candles and kneeling on the pavement beneath the prison walls of the old fortress."

And it was so all the way: thousands upon thousands massed upon their knees and stretching far down the distances, thick-sown with the faint yellow candle-flames, like a field starred with golden flowers.

But there were some that did not kneel; these were the English soldiers. They stood elbow to elbow, on each side of Joan's road, and walled it in all the way; and behind these living walls knelt the multitudes.

By and by a frantic man in priest's garb came wailing and lamenting, and tore through the crowd and the barrier of soldiers and flung himself on his knees by Joan's cart and put up his hands in supplication, crying out:

"O forgive, forgive!"

It was Loyseleur!

And Joan forgave him; forgave him out of a heart that knew nothing but forgiveness, nothing but compassion, nothing but pity for all that suffer, let their offense be what it might. And she had no word of reproach for this poor wretch who had wrought day and night with deceits and treacheries and hypocrisies to betray her to her death.

The soldiers would have killed him, but the Earl of Warwick saved his life. What became of him is not known. He hid himself from the world somewhere, to endure his remorse as he might.

In the square of the Old Market stood the two platforms and the stake that had stood before in the churchyard of St. Ouen. The platforms were occupied as before, the one by Joan and her judges, the other by great dignitaries, the principal being Cauchon and the English Cardinal — Winchester. The square was packed with people, the windows and roofs of the blocks of buildings surrounding it were black with them.

When the preparations had been finished, all noise and movement gradually ceased, and a waiting stillness followed which was solemn and impressive.

And now, by order of Cauchon, an ecclesiastic named Nicholas Midi preached a sermon, wherein he explained that when a branch of the vine — which is the Church — becomes diseased and corrupt, it must be cut away or it will corrupt and destroy the whole vine. He made it appear that Joan, through her wickedness, was a menace and a peril to the Church's purity and holiness, and her death therefore necessary. When he was come to the end of his discourse he turned toward her and paused a moment, then he said:

"Joan, the Church can no longer protect you. Go in peace!'

Joan had been placed wholly apart and conspicuous, to signify the Church's abandonment of her, and she sat there in her loneliness, waiting in patience and resignation for the end. Cauchon addressed her now. He had been advised to read the form of her abjuration to her, and had brought it with him; but he changed his mind, fearing that she would proclaim the truth — that she had never knowingly abjured — and so bring shame upon him and eternal infamy. He contented himself with admonishing her to keep in mind her wickednesses, and repent of them, and think of her salvation. Then he solemnly pronounced her excommunicate and cut off from the body of the Church. With a final word he delivered her over to the secular arm for judgment and sentence.

Joan, weeping, knelt and began to pray. For whom? Herself? Oh, no — for the King of France. Her voice rose sweet and clear, and penetrated all hearts with its passionate pathos. She never thought of his treacheries to her, she never thought of his desertion of her, she never remembered that it was because he was an ingrate that she was here to die a miserable death; she remembered only that he was her King, that she was his loyal and loving subject, and that his enemies had undermined his cause with evil reports and false charges, and he not by to defend himself. And so, in the very presence of death, she forgot her own troubles to implore all in her hearing to be just to him; to believe that he was good and noble and sincere, and not in any way to blame for any acts of hers, neither advising them nor urging them, but being wholly clear and free of all responsibility for them. Then, closing, she begged in humble and touching words that all here present would pray for her and would pardon her, both her enemies and such as might look friendly upon her and feel pity for her in their hearts.

There was hardly one heart there that was not touched — even the English, even the judges showed it, and there was many a lip that trembled and many an eye that was blurred with tears; yes, even the English Cardinal's — that man with a political heart of stone but a human heart of flesh.

The secular judge who should have delivered judgment and pronounced sentence was himself so disturbed that he forgot his duty, and Joan went to her death unsentenced — thus completing with an illegality what had begun illegally and had so continued to the end. He only said — to the guards:

"Take her;" and to the executioner, "Do your duty."

Joan asked for a cross. None was able to furnish one. But an English soldier broke a stick in two and crossed the pieces and tied them together, and this cross he gave her, moved to it by the good heart that was in him; and she kissed it and put it in her bosom. Then Isambard de la Pierre went to the church near by and brought her a consecrated one; and this one also she kissed, and pressed it to her bosom with rapture, and then kissed it again and again, covering it with tears and pouring out her gratitude to God and the saints.

And so, weeping, and with her cross to her lips, she climbed up the cruel steps to the face of the stake, with the friar Isambard at her side. Then she was helped up to the top of the pile of wood that was built around the lower third of the stake, and stood upon it with her back against the stake, and the world gazing up at her breathless. The executioner ascended to her side and wound chains about her slender body, and so fastened her to the stake. Then he descended to finish his dreadful office; and there she remained alone — she that had had so many friends in the days when she was free, and had been so loved and so dear.

All these things I saw, albeit dimly and blurred with tears; but I could bear no more. I continued in my place, but what I shall deliver to you now I got by others' eyes and others' mouths. Tragic sounds there were that pierced my ears and wounded my heart as I sat there, but it is as I tell you: the latest image recorded by my eyes in that desolating hour was Joan of Arc with the grace of her comely youth still unmarred; and that image, untouched by time or decay, has remained with me all my days. Now I will go on.

If any thought that now, in that solemn hour when all transgressors repent and confess, she would revoke her revocation and say her great deeds had been evil deeds and Satan and his fiends their source, they erred. No such thought was in her blameless mind. She was not thinking of herself and her troubles, but of others, and of woes that might befall them. And so, turning her grieving eyes about her, where rose the towers and spires of that fair city, she said:

"Oh, Rouen, Rouen, must I die here, and must you be my tomb? Ah, Rouen, Rouen, I have great fear that you will suffer for my death."

A whiff of smoke swept upward past her face, and for one moment terror seized her and she cried out, "Water! Give me holy water!" but the next moment her fears were gone, and they came no more to torture her.

She heard the flames crackling below her, and immediately distress for a fellow-creature who was in danger took possession of her. It was the friar Isambard. She had given him her cross and begged him to raise it toward her face and let her eyes rest in hope and consolation upon it till she was entered into the peace of God. She made him go out from the danger of the fire. Then she was satisfied, and said:

"Now keep it always in my sight until the end."

Not even yet could Cauchon, that man without shame, endure to let her die in peace, but went toward her, all black with crimes and sins as he was, and cried out:

"I am come, Joan, to exhort you for the last time to repent and seek the pardon of God."

"I die through you," she said, and these were the last words she spoke to any upon earth.

Then the pitchy smoke, shot through with red flashes of flame, rolled up in a thick volume and hid her from sight; and from the heart of this darkness her voice rose strong and eloquent in prayer, and when by moments the wind shredded somewhat of the smoke aside, there were veiled glimpses of an upturned face and moving lips. At last a mercifully swift tide of flame burst upward, and none saw that face any more nor that form, and the voice was still.

Yes, she was gone from us: JOAN OF ARC! What little words they are, to tell of a rich world made empty and poor!

CONCLUSION

JOAN'S brother Jacques died in Domremy during the Great Trial at Rouen. This was according to the prophecy which Joan made that day in the pastures the time that she said the rest of us would go to the great wars.

When her poor old father heard of the martyrdom it broke his heart and he died.

The mother was granted a pension by the city of Orleans, and upon this she lived out her days, which were many. Twenty-four years after her illustrious child's death she traveled all the way to Paris in the winter time and was present at the opening of the discussion in the Cathedral of Nôtre Dame which was the first step in the Rehabilitation. Paris was crowded with people, from all about France, who came to get sight of the venerable dame, and it was a touching spectacle when she moved through these reverend wet-eyed multitudes on her way to the grand honors awaiting her at the cathedral. With her were Jean and Pierre, no longer the light-hearted youths who marched with us from Vaucouleurs, but war-worn veterans with hair beginning to show frost.

After the martyrdom Noël and I went back to Domremy, but presently when the Constable Richemont superseded La Tremouille as the King's chief adviser and began the completion of Joan's great work, we put on our harness and returned to the field and fought for the King all through the wars and skirmishes until France was freed of the English. It was what Joan would have desired of us; and, dead or alive, her desire was law for us. All the survivors of the personal staff were faithful to her memory and fought for the King to the end. Mainly we were well scattered, but when Paris fell we happened to be together. It was a great day and a joyous; but it was a sad one at the same time, because Joan was not there to march into the captured capital with us.

Noël and I remained always together, and I was by his side when death claimed him. It was in the last great battle of the war. In that battle fell also Joan's sturdy old enemy Talbot. He was eighty-five years old, and had spent his whole life in battle. A fine old lion he was, with his flowing white mane and his tameless spirit; yes, and his indestructible energy as well; for he fought as knightly and vigorous a fight that day as the best man there.

La Hire survived the martyrdom thirteen years; and always fighting, of course, for that was all he enjoyed in life. I did not him see in all that time, for we were far apart, but one was always hearing of him.

The Bastard of Orleans and D'Alençon and D'Aulon lived to see France free, and to testify with Jean and Pierre d'Arc and Pasquerel and me at the Rehabilitation. But they are all at rest now, these many years. I alone am left of those who fought at the side of Joan of Arc in the great wars. She said I would live until these wars were forgotten—a prophecy which failed. If I should live a thousand years it would still fail. For whatsoever had touch with Joan of Arc, that thing is immortal.

Members of Joan's family married, and they have left descendants. Their descendants are of the nobility, but their family name and blood bring them honors which no other nobles receive or may hope for. You have seen how everybody along the way uncovered when those children came yesterday to pay their duty to me. It was not because they are noble, it is because they are grandchildren of the brothers of Joan of Arc.

Now as to the Rehabilitation. Joan crowned the King at Rheims. For reward he allowed her to be hunted to her death without making one effort to save her. During the next twenty-three years he remained indifferent to her memory; indifferent to the fact that her good name was under a damning blot put there by the priests because of the deeds which she had done in saving him and his scepter; indifferent to the fact that France was ashamed, and longed to have the Deliverer's fair fame restored. Indifferent all that time. Then he suddenly changed and was anxious to have justice for poor Joan himself. Why? Had he become grateful at last? Had remorse attacked his hard heart? No, he had a better reason—a better one for his sort of man. This better reason was that, now that the English had been finally expelled from the country, they were beginning to call attention to the fact that this King had gotten his crown by the hands of a person proven by the priests to have been in league with Satan and burned for it by them as a sorceress—therefore, of what value or authority was such a Kingship as that? Of no value at all; no nation could afford to allow such a king to remain on the throne.

It was high time to stir now, and the King did it. That is how Charles VII. came to be smitten with anxiety to have justice done the memory of his benefactress.

He appealed to the Pope, and the Pope appointed a great commission of churchmen to examine into the facts of Joan's life and award judgment. The Commission sat at Paris, at Domremy, at Rouen, at Orleans, and at several other places, and continued its work during several months. It examined the records of Joan's trials, it examined the Bastard of Orleans, and the Duke d'Alençon, and D'Aulon, and Pasquerel, and Courcelles, and Isambard de la Pierre, and Manchon, and me, and many others whose names I have made familiar to you; also they examined more than a hundred witnesses whose names are less familiar to you — friends of Joan in Domremy, Vaucouleurs, Orleans, and other places, and a number of judges and other people who had assisted at the Rouen trials, the abjuration, and the martyrdom. And out of this exhaustive examination Joan's character and history came spotless and perfect, and this verdict was placed upon record, to remain forever.

I was present upon most of these occasions, and saw again many faces which I have not seen for a quarter of a century; among them some well-beloved faces — those of our generals and that of Catherine Boucher (married, alas!), and also among them certain other faces that filled me with bitterness — those of Beaupere and Courcelles and a number of their fellow-fiends. I saw Haumette and Little Mengette — edging along toward fifty now, and mothers of many children. I saw Noël's father, and the parents of the Paladin and the Sunflower.

It was beautiful to hear the Duke d'Alençon praise Joan's splendid capacities as a general, and to hear the Bastard indorse these praises with his eloquent tongue and then go on and tell how sweet and good Joan was, and how full of pluck and fire and impetuosity, and mischief, and mirthfulness, and tenderness, and compassion, and everything that was pure and fine and noble and lovely. He made her live again before me, and wrung my heart.

I have finished my story of Joan of Arc, that wonderful child, that sublime personality, that spirit which in one regard has had no peer and will have none — this: its purity from all alloy of self-seeking, self-interest, personal ambition. In it no trace of these motives can be found, search as you may, and this cannot be said of any other person whose name appears in profane history.

With Joan of Arc love of country was more than a sentiment — it was a passion. She was the Genius of Patriotism — she was Patriotism embodied, concreted, made flesh, and palpable to the touch and visible to the eye.

Love, Mercy, Charity, Fortitude, War, Peace, Poetry, Music — these may be symbolized as any shall prefer: by figures of either sex and of any age; but a slender girl in her first young bloom, with the martyr's crown upon her head, and in her hand the sword that severed her country's bonds — shall not this, and no other, stand for PATRIOTISM through all the ages until time shall end?